MW00679589

FOR

*The book in your hands could
never tell all my mother's heart
wants to say to you about life,
love, friendship, fulfillment and,
most important of all, the Lord's
reality. But as you read, I pray
you'll be encouraged, and that
you are reminded how very special you are to me and what
marvelous plans God has for you.
I pray that what is shared here
will help you grow into confident
womanhood, a joy-filled life and
an eternity of enjoying God.*

WITH LOVE FROM

ON THIS DAY.

My Wish for You

Blessings for Daughters

Cheri Fuller and
Sandra Picklesimer Aldrich

VINE BOOKS
SERVANT PUBLICATIONS
ANN ARBOR, MICHIGAN

Vine Books is an imprint of Servant Publications especially designed
to serve evangelical Christians.

Published in association with the literary agency of Alive
Communications, Inc., 1465 Kelly Johnson Blvd., Suite 320, Colorado
Springs, CO 80920.

Published by Servant Publications
P.O. Box 8617
Ann Arbor, Michigan 48107

Cover design: PAZ Design Group, Salem, Oregon

00   01   02   03   10   9   8   7   6   5   4   3   2   1

Printed in the United States of America
ISBN 1-56955-132-4

Cataloging-in-Publication Data on file at the Library of Congress.

For three special young women who bless my life,
Alison Plum, Tiffany Fuller and Maggie Fuller

- - - - - - - - -

Cheri

Dedication

For two favorite young women,
Holly Aldrich Hulen
and
Marianne Reddin Aldrich

- - - - - - - - -

Sandra

Contents

A word to moms and daughters

11. I wish for you happiness ... but not at the expense of holiness.

12. I wish for you a heart of prayer ... and ears that hear the Father's voice.

13. I wish for you to know when to say "No" ... and when to say "Yes!"

14. I wish for you to love the Lord ... and to express that love to others.

15. I wish for you to really like yourself ... and to be proud of who God has made you.

16. I wish for you a way to express yourself ... to reflect the unique creation God intended you to be.

17. I wish for you to be able to tell the truth ... and to hear it gracefully.

18. I wish for you an active, energetic lifestyle ... now and for the rest of your life.

19. I wish for you to see the best in others ... without being blind to their weaknesses.

20. I wish for you not to put off joy ... but to celebrate life today and every day.

21. My wish for you ... *a special letter from me to you.*

A word to moms and daughters ...

T his book is, pure and simple, a labor of love. We know what you're going through right now.

In our teens, we too couldn't wait to be free of parental limitations and restrictions. We'd hide in our bedrooms, listen to music and count the days until we could move out. Leaving home was to be a much-anticipated, breathless flight of wonder.

In our twenties we discovered that, while coming home to visit wasn't the same as living there, it still felt secure and good. We were sometimes loath to admit that in our zealous quest for independence. And yet, when Mom and Dad took down our trophies and stuffed animals and turned our rooms into offices and craft rooms, they heard about it for weeks!

In our thirties, we looked back on our youth with a mixture of embarrassment and longing, and wished we had known as much then as we do now. Such wisdom was bought at a price, of course. The fine "laugh lines" around our eyes bear positive proof we have weathered a few storms. But the truth is, we wouldn't go back for a moment. Not even for a date with the captain of the football team.

As you take that plunge into the "real world," we'd like to spare you some of life's more painful lessons. In truth, some lessons can really only be learned firsthand ... but others, we hope, can be shared vicariously. This book contains our hopes for you, the blessings we pray will be yours in the coming years.

The last chapter in this book is a blank "wish." Moms, you can be as creative as you like with those pages.... Add quotes or Scriptures that you have found especially meaningful over the years, or even write a wish or two of your own!

Daughters, you can add to these pages, too. Every year we earn a few more "experience coins" to add to our storehouse of wisdom. If some of these blessings don't seem very valuable right now, set them aside. You may need them later.

It is our deepest wish, however, that you will never set aside the One who loves you most of all. He goes with you, even when we can't be there. May He give you all the joy and happiness your heart can hold.

**I wish for you to treasure
your friendships …
*and to be
a treasured friend.***

*Many people
will walk in
and out of your
life. But only
true friends will
leave footprints
in your heart.*
ANONYMOUS

"Make new friends, but
keep the old. One is sil-
ver and the other, gold," we sang
in Girl Scouts. But it's just as true
today; perhaps even more so. We
need treasured friendships that
we cultivate, enjoy and appreci-
ate. Even wonderful, intimate
relationships with husbands and
children do not eliminate
our need for
friendships with
other women.
In fact, it is
often *because*
of those
friendships that we
are able to give our best
selves to those closest
to us.

"We all need one or two real friends in whom we can confide the deepest yearnings of our hearts. We all need companionship. We need someone to whom we don't have to explain ourselves. Someone who 'gets' our humor, who loves us even when we are unlovely. Someone upon whom we can depend in times of crisis," said beloved Christian author Eugenia Price. Eugenia's associate, Rosalind Rinker, was that kind of friend, especially during a particularly difficult year when Eugenia's father's was critically ill. "She prayed with me. She prayed with Mother. She helped us get our hasty meals together. She let me talk and talk at night after long hours at the hospital, when I was too upset to sleep. She was there in all ways. She was a real friend. And if ever I needed a friend, I needed one during those endless days and weeks while my beloved dad lay dying in a hospital."[1]

The important thing was that although their friendship was on a permanent, easy, secure basis, it was not centered in just the two women. It was centered in Jesus Christ. "I am not her security and she is not mine. He is *our* security. We can fail each other but He will never fail us."[2]

We may have many associates, coworkers, neighbors and acquaintances, but only a few heart-to-heart soul mates who will last throughout our whole life. Anne of Green Gables called this kind of friend a "kindred spirit": someone with whom we can easily cry, laugh and just *be*, maybe quite comfortably without exchanging any words.

God doesn't give us scores of these "golden friends." That's why we should treat them with such care. Such friendships don't just happen; treasured ones take effort. "It costs to be a friend, or to have a friend: there is nothing else in life, except motherhood, that costs so much. It costs time, affection, strength, patience, love."[3]

In your lifetime you may live in a number of different places—mobility is a fact of life in this day and age. You may have to move far away from the friends you love most. But as you pack your boxes to move to another city or state, be careful not to mentally dispose of the deep friendships you are leaving behind.

Weed out the clothes you no longer wear. Give away any household items you no longer use. Just don't let miles stand in the way of friendship or break your bond of love. It may take energy and creativity, but keep cultivating your relationship, and you'll find the blessings of a lasting friendship are more than worth the effort.

Nine months after Papa died, Mama sold the house we'd lived in and moved us to McCommas Street, which meant starting a new school, Stonewall Jackson Elementary. The first week, as I was wandering through the halls, I met Mary Jaynes (now Mayer). We were both in seventh grade, and before long we were best friends.

There is an old saying: "A loyal friend is like a safe

To discover a kindred spirit is to find your heart abiding in the heart of a friend.

ANN PARRISH

shelter; find one and you have found a treasure." God knew I needed a shelter at that time, while dealing with the loss of my father and some turmoil at home. Everything was changing, and the shelter of her friendship provided shade for my wounded heart. Mary's family adopted me into their circle of love, and I have wonderful memories of that difficult year because of them.

Mary lived on a small lake, and we spent Saturday afternoons paddling around in her paddle boat, brown bag lunches in hand. Even a trip to the local drugstore to look at greeting cards could turn into a hilarious afternoon because we found exactly the same cards funny. Mary and I double-dated (with parents driving, of course) to ballroom dancing school, camped out in her backyard and played cards until late at night. One summer her family even took me on their family vacation to New Mexico and Colorado.

After the seventh grade, because of the dividing lines the school district had set, Mary had to go to a different junior high than I did. A year after that, my mother remarried and we moved again—to a small town outside the city. Still, Mary and I made an effort to keep up our friendship. Later we roomed together in college and were bridesmaids in each other's weddings.

In the past thirty years, we have never once lived in the same city, but our friendship has held fast. We have exchanged countless letters, shared photos of our children and wept with each other when our mothers died. This Christmas Mary and her husband Jim flew here to attend our son Chris' wedding, and we have get-togethers planned for next year.

Mary and I haven't been able to see each other as much as we would have liked. And yet, because of Mary I've learned a few secrets about how to develop a lasting friendship.

Write letters. Mary and I have kept up a lively correspondence over the years, and it makes my day to see a flower-bordered envelope with her handwriting in my mailbox. Writing letters keeps you heart-to-heart even when you're not in the same location. It's not exactly like chatting over lunch together, but sometimes I have a favorite cup of raspberry tea while I read Mary's newsy letter and enjoy it immensely.

Yes, just lately we've begun to e-mail each other, and that's great. You can get much quicker response to your questions. You can send instant "SOS" requests for your friend's prayers and save money on stamps. But keep those "real" letters and notes coming, for they are some of the delights of a long-distance friendship. These reminders of friendship can be tucked away in your Bible or journal and brought out on gray days when you need some encouraging words.

Be thoughtful. Remembering your friend at birthdays

and Christmas is a nice way of saying, "I'm thinking about you. I care." And it doesn't have to be expensive, store-bought gifts you exchange. One of my favorite gifts ever from Mary is a handmade grandmother quilt Mary created when our first grandbaby, Caitlin, was born. Whenever I get it out and spread the quilt on the floor for Caitlin to play on, I'm reminded of Mary's friendship, a covering of love that has spanned the years.

Plan getaways. Whenever possible, plan a once-a-year in-person visit with your friend where you can have long lunches, strolls, shopping or other fun, and most important, an extended chance to catch up on each other's lives. When I lived in Yarmouth, Maine, for two years and Mary had just moved to Chicago, we left the kids at home with the dads, met in Boston and enjoyed a terrific weekend of sightseeing, complete with high tea at a lovely old Boston hotel. We've even met halfway between Dallas and Oklahoma City just to have a meal together. Be creative and find a way to get together even if you live hundreds of miles away from each other. You'll pick up your conversation as if you'd never been apart, and both of your souls will be refreshed from the good fellowship.

Pray for each other. Nothing connects us with a friend like praying for each other's needs. You could trade prayer lists weekly, like my two friends Cynthia and Karen, or designate a day each week or month that you focus special prayers of blessing on each other and each other's families. Using the letters B-L-E-S-S, you can pray five blessings for your friend:

Body—blessings for her health, protection, strength
Labor—blessings on her work and ministry, both in and out of the home
Emotional—joy, peace, hope
Social—love, marriage, family, friends
Spiritual—salvation, faith, grace[4]

Just as friendship must extend across the miles, so it must also bridge the changing circumstances of life. When you get engaged or are newly married, don't leave your friends—including your single ones—in the dust. It's easy to get so wrapped up in the bliss and excitement over the guy you've dreamed of that you exclude old friends from your life. Instead, offer hospitality; meet for lunch; keep in touch by phone. Whether you change last names or addresses, don't leave a string of broken or neglected friendships behind you.

While you cherish and cultivate old friendships, always be open to new ones. While we cherish our golden friendships, sometimes God surprises us with a new or "silver" friend. Some may be very different from you. She may be ten years older or younger than you, married or single, at-home mom or career woman. Keep your heart open to all the friendships

God has for you, at every stage of life.

In heaven we'll make new friends, I believe, but we'll also be reunited with those "golden" friends. And this time, we'll all have the same address.

CHERI FULLER

To have a friend is to have one of the sweetest gifts that life can bring: to be a friend is to have a solemn and tender education of soul from day to day. A friend gives us confidence for life. A friend remembers us when we have forgotten ourselves, or neglected ourselves.

ANNA ROBERTSON BROWN[5]

1. Eugenia Price, *Woman to Woman* (New York: Harper Paperbacks, Zondervan, 1959), 166.
2. Price, 166.
3. Anna Robertson Brown, "What Is Worthwhile?" a paper read before the Philadelphia Branch of the Association of Collegiate Alumnae, 6.
4. Adapted from the brochure "Five Blessings" (Grand Rapids, Mich.: HOPE [Houses of Prayer Everywhere, 800-217-5200]), 1.
5. Brown, 6.

**I wish for you to explore
the world fearlessly …
*and to know
the danger zones.***

Rachel agreed to go on her
youth group's mission tour—
and hated every minute of it. She
griped about the heat and dust.
She complained that the local
people stared at her clothing. She
groaned when reminded that a
morning shower was limited to
five minutes. She whined over
the lumpy bed. And she complained about each national food
dish on the table. "Why
can't these people do
things the right
way?"

Finally the team
leader took her
aside. "Rachel,
these people

*I always told
the Lord, "I
trust You. I
don't know
where to go or
what to do, but
I expect You to
lead me," and
He always did.*

HARRIET TUBMAN

are not wrong; they're just *different.* You have come into *their* land. You can't expect them to act as though they are from your country. How would you feel if they visited our town and complained we weren't doing things the right way?"

His words hit their target, and for the rest of the trip Rachel limited her complaints to occasional sighs and quiet vows that she would never again travel beyond U.S. borders.

I like my familiar comforts, too. But like Rachel's youth leader, I discovered that there is a big difference between "wrong" and "different."

Think about the way Jesus healed people. He didn't limit Himself to only one "correct" way of healing. Sometimes He healed with a *touch,* as when He touched the hand of Peter's mother-in-law (see Mt 8:15) or the leper (see Mk 1:41).

Sometimes He *spoke.* He commanded the man with the shriveled hand to stretch it out (see Mk 3:5); He commanded demons out of a man and into a nearby swine herd (see Mk 5:8, 13).

Sometimes He *sent His healing ahead.* When the centurion asked for healing for his servant at home, Jesus healed the servant without even seeing him (see Mt 8:13)!

Sometimes Jesus healed people in even stranger ways. In John 9 He spit into the dirt to make a mud paste for the blind man's eyes. I confess I don't like *that* miracle. It just isn't my definition of how Jesus *should* heal.... But then, I have to ask myself: Could I be over-looking or even refusing God's miracles in my own life, just because they didn't come in the "correct" package?

This is a wonderful world we live in, full of colors and textures and experiences God meant for us to enjoy. Be open to the new and different.

At the same time, remember that different isn't always better. I'm thinking of Peggy, who calls herself a free spirit just because she refuses to arrive on time for meetings, is annoyed by traffic laws, complains about conventional rules of etiquette and ignores com-monsense guidelines. In some ways it might be tempt-ing to follow her example, to live life on my own terms. However, my first visit to the Middle East reminded me of the importance of balancing a sense of adventure with *common* sense.

A confident world traveller, I foolishly had decided to do a bit of exploring—away from our group. Drawn by the intrigues of Old Jerusalem, I walked two miles beyond the usual tourist area before I discovered that I was almost out of water in an area where no one spoke English. I tried using every foreign word I could remember for *water*, beginning with the Spanish word *agua*. Of course, my Spanish was just as useless as my English in the heart of the Israeli town.

Finally, I leaned against a low stone fence to ponder my situation. There in my obvious American tourist garb, I felt a pebble hit my back. Then another. And another.

Knowing any display of fear might incite the thrower to become even more aggressive, I stood up slowly and gathered my canvas bag holding the now-empty water bottle. As I made my way back up the lane with what I hoped was a confident stride, I quoted Psalm 91:11 to myself: "For he will command his angels concerning you to guard you in all your ways."

Lord, I know I was foolhardy to come here, I silently prayed, *but I ask that Your angel guard me right now. And if angels can choose any form they want, I'd like to request one that's about 6'8" with long hair held back by a don't-mess-with-me bandanna.*

Then picturing my new, unseen companion by my side, I confidently walked the two miles back to the group, arriving thirsty but wiser.

As you are finding your balance between different and wrong, unconventional and foolhardy, remember that you will never be able to please everyone. The ancient storyteller Aesop emphasized this point in one of my favorite fables:

One fine spring morning, a father and his son were on their way to town market, leading their donkey, which would carry their purchases home, and enjoying the beautiful morning together.

On the way, they met one of their neighbors who said, "How silly of you both to walk when you have such a fine donkey."

So the father set his son on the donkey, and they continued toward the market, still talking and enjoying the morning.

But just as they came to a bend in the road, they met another neighbor returning from town, who glared at the son and said, "How rude you are to ride while your old father must walk."

So the child slid down from the donkey's back, the father climbed on and they continued toward town.

But just as they topped a little hill, they were met by yet another neighbor who scowled at the father and said, "What a selfish father you are to make this dear child walk, while you, a grown man, ride."

So the father pulled his son up to sit in front of him on the donkey's back. Of course, it wasn't long before they met a fourth neighbor.

"How cruel you are," he said, "to make this poor donkey carry the two of you to town."

So they both slid off the donkey, and the strong father promptly picked up the animal and put it across his shoulders.

As they walked along, still talking and still enjoying the day, they met another neighbor, who doubled over with laughter. "That is the most stupid thing I've ever seen! Donkeys are to be ridden, not carried!"

Yes, there's a fine line between doing what is truly

right and what is merely local custom, between what is wrong and what is merely different. But as you prayerfully allow yourself to move outside of your usual comfort areas, you will find excitement and challenge—and greater awareness of God's great creativity.

Three

I wish for you a heart that yearns for the One who made you … *that you would seek not only His hand, but His face.*

*B*ut we all,
with unveiled face beholding as in a mirror the glory of the Lord, are being transformed into the same image from glory to glory, just as from the Lord, the Spirit.

2 CORINTHIANS 3:18,
NASB

Life can be full of problems. Sometimes it seems as though just when one set of problems is resolved, another set comes around the corner. Yet I've learned that attitude and perspective—how we respond or react to our problems—affect the outcome as much as circumstances themselves.

God has taught me important lessons through my greatest life challenges. The times I've learned the most, though, have been when my thoughts were moved from the problem

(whether it was mildly distressing or overwhelming) to something He revealed to me about Himself. Seeing a glimpse of God's character and nature, focusing on His sufficiency or how able He is, made all the difference.

I remember when we were about to move from the first home we'd ever owned, a little house that I was very fond of. I loved the yellow print kitchen wallpaper and the way we'd fixed up the nursery, and the young mothers in the neighborhood had become close friends.

This had been my "comfort zone," the first place that I had really felt at home in our marriage. "Lord, you know I don't like moving and change. I'd be happy and content if we just stayed put and didn't even move the furniture around." I continued to pour out my sad feelings, but before long, I heard His still, small voice saying, "But I'm your dwelling place, not the house you live in. You can always feel at home if you abide in Me. You'll have other houses to live in temporarily, but I'm your real dwelling place!"

As I thought about that amazing idea, I suddenly felt a peace in knowing He'd be with us wherever we were. He'd never leave us or forsake us (see Heb 13:5), and someday when I got to heaven, I wouldn't have to move ever again! Getting my focus back on God and who He is, instead of the changing circumstances, sustained me through not just one but many moves.

So one of my prayers and hopes for you is that you'll develop a God-ward focus, an attitude toward life much like the one David demonstrates in the Psalms. Though he expressed all his emotions (fear, complaints, grief, cries for help, etc.) to God when he was facing terrible problems, *he always refocused on God Himself*—His character, His lovingkindness and faithfulness—lifting up His name in praise no matter what the distress or trial was.

Something Anne Graham Lotz said about this struck me: "Sometimes, when faced with great problems, our tendency is to focus on the hand of God—what He has not done for us, and what we want Him to do for us— instead of focusing on the face of God, simply *who He is*. Often in the midst of great problems, we stop short of the real blessing God has for us, which is a fresh vision of who He is. When we stop focusing on our problems or ourselves and focus instead on our Almighty and Omnipresent God, our problems, as the old hymn promises, 'grow strangely dim in the light of His glory and grace.'"[1]

What she's describing is a lifestyle of praise that doesn't mean you deny your real feelings. It's expressing your whole range of emotions to God yet choosing to keep praising Him in spite of how things look to you—and not postponing worship until you feel better.

How can you develop this kind of attitude that is

beyond our feelings, that will help us keep our eyes on God even in storms and stresses that may come?

First, make a conscious effort to look up to the Lord. Even Amy Carmichael, who for more than fifty-five years rescued thousands of Indian children from destruction and abuse in the Hindu temples, experienced what it was like to get caught in the crush of life and pushed down. She advised us, "If you get overwhelmed or feel like you're under the circumstances, the next thing we know is that we are groveling in the dust. Things are on the top of us; we are not on the top of anything. So God calls us, 'Look from the top' (see Sg 4:8). He's saying, 'Come with me from all that, come up the mountain with Me and look from the top.'"

In everyday life, Carmichael said, "The Lord Jesus ... is our Peace, our Victory, and our Joy.... From below, things feel impossible, people seem impossible (some people at least), and we ourselves feel most impossible of all. From the top we see as our Lord sees: He sees not what is only, but what shall be. He is not discouraged, and as we look with Him, our discouragement vanishes, and we can sing a new song."[2]

Next, focus on God's name and His attributes. Psalm 9:10 says, "Those who know your name will trust in you, for you, Lord, have never forsaken those who seek you." That means when we or a loved one has a broken heart or a body that needs mending, we can praise Jehovah-Rapha, the Great Physician who came to heal the brokenhearted and touch those who need His help. When our homes are filled with irritation and stress, we can focus on the Prince of Peace and invite Him into our midst. Then as we pray, we know we aren't asking something outside His character, and our confidence in God's ability to handle things, increase.

All through the Bible, God gives us snapshots of Himself; He reveals Himself through His dealings with people, and describing His attributes could fill a library. Each week when I begin the prayer group I lead, we begin with praising God for something about His character or who He is. As I've done this for a number of years, I've found we'll never run out of attributes! Try it and you'll see. Start with A and then proceed through the alphabet with a concordance and Bible and find an attribute for each letter.

When you go through trials, ask God, "What do you

want to reveal to me about Yourself, Lord? What are you trying to teach me?" As you pay attention to the glimpses and whispers from God, you'll see Him more and more clearly. You'll receive the real blessing He has for you in all seasons and in every trial—a fresh vision of who He is!

1. Anne Graham Lotz, "A Fresh Vision of God" in *One Holy Passion*, ed. Judy Couchman (Colorado Springs: Waterbrook, 1998), 75–76.
2. Amy Carmichael, *Edges of His Ways* (Fort Washington, Pa.: Christian Literature Crusade, 1988), 175.

Four

**I wish for you the wisdom of experience ...
*and the inner strength to find it.***

You are of God, little children, and have overcome them, because He who is in you is greater than he who is in the world.

1 JOHN 4:4, NKJV

You can be anything you want to be, if you're willing to work for it: teacher, writer, mother, doctor, missionary or any number of equally worthy pursuits. However, being successful in life—and especially at being a faithful follower of Christ—takes a dogged perseverance, because the path of most goals worth reaching is strewn with obstacles and setbacks. And it's awfully easy to quit in discouragement before you reach the end! Florence Chadwick's experience has something to say to us about this.

Many years ago (in 1952 to be exact) Florence, the long-distance swim champion of the world, was set to swim the channel from the California coast to Catalina Island. She'd been the first woman to ever swim the English Channel, so long-distance swimming wasn't new to her. But the morning Florence dove in the water for the forty-six-mile swim, it was foggy and overcast. The water was chilling and the fog so thick she could barely see the boats around her. The waters were infested with sharks so that her trainers on the accompanying boats had to use rifles to drive them away. For fifteen hours Florence swam, braving the numbing cold and the sharks, but her discouragement grew. Finally she could go no farther, and she asked her trainers to lift her into the boat. They encouraged her to keep swimming since they could see they were close to land, but all she could see was the fog.

Florence quit. And when she got into the boat, she saw she was only a half mile from the shore. She had stopped within sight of her destination.

Sometimes we become shrouded in a fog of discouragement or weariness, and it looks as if things will never change. But Florence's experience reminds us to not give up too soon. Keep praying. Gather others around you to help you persevere. The breakthrough may be just around the corner.

When I think of perseverance, I'm reminded of a woman named Miss Mitchell, a missionary to India. When Miss Mitchell left for India, it was the high point in her life. Serving Christ in this foreign country was a dream come true, an assignment the young woman had prayed and planned for and definitely felt God called her to.

However, when she arrived in India, she was overwhelmed by culture shock, not only by the Indian culture but also because of the house to which she was assigned. It was the home of two older missionaries who were totally devoted to their mission work. She couldn't add her own touches to make it feel homey. And with everyone so busy, there was no time for fellowship, sharing or anything else, and she grew desperately lonely.

Other problems soon surfaced: Miss Mitchell had difficulty with the language and even began to dislike the sight of the Indian people to whom she'd come to share Christ. Quite unhappy, she greatly desired a husband, children and home of her own.

The last blow came when she fell ill with amoebic dysentery. The doctor said her recovery and very survival depended on leaving India. It seemed her ministry was coming to a disappointing end.

She hated to let God down and admit failure. But overcome with discouragement, Miss Mitchell began packing to go home. The very morning she was scheduled to leave for the United States, she read in her quiet time from Joshua 10.

In this passage, five enemy kings fled in the heat of battle to the cave at Makkedah, to hide from Joshua's men. When the kings were discovered, Joshua boldly ordered stones to be rolled to the mouth of the cave to seal the kings inside. Later, he told his captains to put their feet on the necks of the five doomed kings before they were put to death.

"Fear not," Miss Mitchell read, "nor be dismayed, be strong and of good courage: for thus shall the Lord do to all your enemies against whom ye fight" (Jos 10:25, KJV).

Reading those words, the young missionary realized immediately she also had five enemies that threatened to end her service in India: her illness, her problem learning the language, her lack of love for the native people, her desire for a husband and a home and her desperate homesickness.

Instead of quitting, Miss Mitchell decided that just as Joshua asserted God's authority over his enemies, she needed to assert her authority in Christ over her enemies. She wrote each of these enemies on a piece of paper—the dysentery, the language problems, homesickness, etc. Then, to symbolize her decision to take authority over each of them, she put her foot on one after another, proclaiming her trust in her all-powerful, resurrected Lord to defeat them.

She promptly unpacked and began to get her focus back on God by spending time praising Him instead of complaining about her problems. She found a teacher to help improve her language skills. Within a week the young woman recovered from her illness. Her language skills gradually but steadily improved. In a short time she got so involved in her ministry that she forgot her homesickness and came to develop a real heart of love for the Indian people. A young man in the region eventually proposed, and she and her family spent many years in a fruitful, fulfilling ministry.

Just like the missionary, you will face things that may tempt you to quit as well. But whether it's Algebra II you're struggling to master or a job that gives you trouble, don't give up. When you face even the toughest problems of life and are tempted to throw in the towel, dear daughter, tie a knot and hang on. Like Miss Mitchell did and as Ephesians 6:13 advises, after you have done all—stand!

**I wish for you
to find love …
*and to live contentedly
until it finds you.***

W*e must not
fall into
the confusion
of mistaking
normal alone-
ness, which is
intended to
draw us to God,
with loneliness.*

EUGENIA PRICE

Molly enjoyed her job in the customer service department of a major publishing company, was active in her church and loved her extended family of nieces and nephews. But even with her ever-present smile, she was growing tired of hearing favorite aunts, coworkers and even strangers ask, "You are such a lovely young woman. Why aren't you married?"

The truth is, she was starting to wonder that herself. *Yes, what is wrong with me?* she thought as she tried not to watch couples holding hands, laughing over din-ner, looking at fur-

niture together. For long moments each morning and evening she stared into the mirror, pondering what she could change that might make her more attractive. Maybe if she lost weight ... or changed her hair color ... or worked more on the leg machine at the gym. Suddenly her life goals were narrowed to this: Get a man! And that meant everything else was put on hold.

Even when three of the young women from her department invited her to join them for a long week-end at a popular tourist spot two hours away, Molly refused, claiming a busy schedule. Actually, she had heard so many good things about the resort that she was determined to save the experience to share with her future husband.

During a going-out-of-business sale at a nearby household store, she passed up incredible savings on her favorite china pattern, saying, *I'll wait until I'm married so we can choose our pattern together.* And, of course, she would never consider buying her own townhouse, even though several in her complex became available at a lower-than-market price the week that particular landlord decided to move to Arizona.

Do you know anyone who is putting her life on hold until she meets "Mr. Right"? The problem with this is twofold. First of all, those who do this rob themselves of today's joy. Psalm 118:24 invites us: "This is the day the Lord has made; let us rejoice and be glad in it."

Secondly, this kind of attitude can create unrealistic expectations about married life. How can one person,

If you bring your own goals and dreams and self-awareness to a marriage, the other person can be a tremendous source of comfort and support. If you bring to the relationship nothing but your neediness, the balance is all off.

DR. LAURA SCHLESSINGER

no matter how wonderful, make up for years of "wasted time"? It's far too much pressure to put on anyone. It's far better to grab the joy of each new day, and to concentrate on *being* the right person instead of *looking* for the right person.

As the months and years rolled by, Mr. Wonderful still did not show up and Molly grew more and more despondent. As the days turned into weeks, she began to panic, thinking, *What if I never get married?* And sadly, any new man who did cross her path would sense her desperation and run rather than give that relationship a chance.

Too bad she didn't know Joanne, a young women who lived on the other side of her townhouse complex. Joanne had jumped at the opportunity to purchase one of the suddenly available units and bought paint—peach for the bedroom, cream and blue for the kitchen—the same afternoon she ordered new drapes.

> *Sometimes relinquishment means giving up a cherished dream, a plan, an illusion. Life is often a series of adjustments—fitting our dreams to reality*
>
> RUTH SENTER

She was looking forward someday to getting married, too, but she wasn't about to miss a great opportunity like this one.

Joanne understood the importance of rejoicing in *this* day. She had also learned from her older sisters that even when Mr. Wonderful finally does show up, it doesn't mean the marriage is going to be perfect. Joanne had learned the "Three Cs" guidelines for dating: companionship, common interests and commitment. She resolved not to be like her couch-potato cousin, who had joined a Saturday hiking club just to snag a man. Two months after the wedding, the cousin had discarded her hiking boots and settled into her old routine of watching videos of 1950s movies, to the great disappointment of her new husband. Sadly, their relationship did not improve.

Along reality's road, Joanne also had learned to get to know the families of those she dated. She knew that no marriage exists in a vacuum—in a sense, you marry the entire family. One of Joanne's sisters makes it a habit before leaving for an extended family gathering to pray, "Lord, help me keep my mouth shut." (She explains, "You never have to apologize for the ugly things you *don't* say!")

Joanne recognizes that both single life and married life have pros and cons. So she has determined not to put off living—and enjoying—*today* just because she's hoping to meet her future husband *tomorrow*. "This is the day the Lord has made; let us rejoice and be glad in it."

Remember: The best surprises often come your way when you least expect them.

Six

**I wish for you a heart
for your home …**
*a place that
expresses who you are
and welcomes those
around you.*

*T*he size of
one's home
should never
dictate the out-
reach of one's
heart.

LUCI SWINDOLL

Edith Schaeffer, the beloved
Christian writer, married her
husband Francis in the summer
between college and his beginning
theological seminary. It was during
the Great Depression; the couple
had no money and jobs were
almost nonexistent. That first summer the Schaeffers spent as
counselors at a camp in
Michigan. Their combined
salary for the whole sea-
son was only $30 plus
room and board.

What were they going
to do for furniture? How
could they make a homey
place out of the little room they

lived in? From wedding money, they had purchased a sewing machine and a table. They had pottery dishes Edith had collected by visiting the "seconds" room of a pottery factory in college. They found an old nail keg in a hardware store, which they padded, covered and remade into a stool. Edith sewed a bedspread and curtains, and they placed some copper candlesticks on their table so they could have tea or supper by candlelight. They made other furniture with their "finds" and "treasures," even a couch with a car seat and springs Francis had found.

Together they created more than a temporary makeshift place—with very little, they were making a home for those few short months. And in each place the Schaeffers lived—from a crowded little chalet in Switzerland when they began L'Abri ministry to the apartment near the Minnesota hospital where Francis received chemotherapy during his last months of life— they made a center of meaningful living and personal enrichment wherever they were, and invited others to share what they had.

In these days of fast-forward living and mobility, it's easy for the places we live to become just pit stops to microwave something to eat and change clothes between work and our evening's activities. And if you're living "temporary," it's a challenge to create a sense of home. But even in a dorm room, duplex or apartment, you can bring your personality, uniqueness and creativity in to create a home. This is just as important when you're single as it is when you're married. Here are some ways to do that:

Surround yourself with the stuff you love. Think about: *What makes me feel at home? Am I surrounded by things that have meaning and depth?* For example, my single friend Connie's apartment sitting room has colorful quilts her grandmother made stacked in a big willow basket. Favorite books fill her two bookshelves. "A house isn't a home without magazines and books to read," Connie tells me. A big, unusual salt rock her sister gave her perches on top of the bookshelf. A delicate wreath Connie created with dried flowers graces the wall. Color, antique lamps, flowers and a green plant round out Connie's room, inviting you to come in, shed your shoes, sink in the comfy chair and join her in reading or chatting.

Don't think you have to wait for marriage to have a home. The real tendency of lots of young women is to think, "Home is where my parents live. I'll have one *someday* when I have a husband and children." Remember, wherever *you* live is your home and it will be what you make it.

Instead of pining over your "someday" home, as Edith Schaeffer says, "Stop dreaming! Make the place where you *live* a place where you are expressing your own taste right now. But also start collecting some things which will continue to be used throughout life, and will be *your* familiar 'things' that will give you continuity."[1] She even advises brides who must spend the

> *Happy is the home that shelters a friend.*
>
> RALPH WALDO EMERSON

first months of marriage some-what mobile to start homemaking in a hotel, rather than moaning about having to "wait so long to have a home."[2]

Paint and fix up now, not later! When renting or even buy-ing a house, don't wait until you're putting it on the market to hang pictures, hang wallpaper and complete all those projects that would make the place look more livable and comfortable. Don't wait until everything's perfect or until you have a bigger dining room to invite friends over for a meal. Fresh paint and family and friends' photos hung on a special wall, having a place for hospitality—do it when you move in so you can *enjoy* the place you live now and for as long as you're there.

Then if and when you do walk down the aisle and become "Mrs."—and later, "Mom"—I pray for you a heart for your home. May you delight in cooking for your husband, children and friends. May you find joy in ministering to them when they're sick, reading and playing with children and nurturing them spiritually. May the beauty and order of your home touch all the senses and create a joyful environment.

It's easy to be so job or ministry focused or have our priorities so set on outside activities that we neglect our homes or have nothing left to give our families. And yet, it is a great calling to be a "home maker," to create order and loveliness, warm hospitality and cherished memories. If we spend all our energies elsewhere, we will miss the incredible ministry within the four walls of our own homes.

"Let your home be your parish, your little brood your congregation, your living room a sanctuary, and your knee a sacred altar," said Billy Graham.

Tip: There's nothing better than walking in from school or work and smelling vegetable soup simmering or bread baking—and the new, easy bread machines put out a delicious aroma. And even if you're working part- or full-time or are busy all day with toddlers, you can start a meal earlier in the day in a crockpot. Later add store-bought or homemade French bread and salad in a bag and *voilà!*—a lovely meal for you, your family and even a few friends.

1. Edith Schaeffer, *Hidden Art* (Wheaton, Ill.: Tyndale House, 1971), 69–70.
2. Schaeffer, 81.

Seven

**I wish for you
independence ...
*and to know when
to ask for help.***

*We work, we
pull, we
struggle, and we
plan until we're
utterly exhaust-
ed, but we have
forgotten to plug
in to the source
of power. And
that source of
power is prayer.*
EVELYN CHRISTENSON

Cassie prided herself on having come from a long line of
strong, independent women, starting with her great-grandmother
who had kept her family of five
fed and clothed even during the
Depression of the 1930s. Then
when Cassie's history professor
talked about the development of
the B-17 bomber that
allowed the
United States
to win World
War II, she
thought of her
grandmother's
twelve-hour shifts
of riveting metal in the nose
of those planes at the Boeing
plant in Seattle. Her own
mother had

been part of the first Peace Corps team that went into West Africa during a 1960s epidemic.

Cassie was carrying on that same strong reputation. She could balance her own checkbook, change the oil in her car and figure her own taxes. And all that while running the computer software company that had grown from three employees to more than a hundred—within the first five years of existence. Cassie demanded a lot from her employees, but she was hardest on herself. In fact, she lived by one philosophy: "If you want something done right; do it yourself." And she acted out that philosophy by double-checking everything her secretary sent out, calling her department managers several times a day and always asking for detailed reports of each step of a new project.

Her favorite historical figure was Molly Ludwig Hayes, the young wife who had followed her husband to the Revolutionary War—and the one whom the soldiers called "Molly Pitcher" as she courageously carried water to the wounded and dying, even during battle. During one particularly fierce attack, Molly saw her husband fall beside the cannon he was firing. She ran to his side—not to cradle him in her arms but to take his place and fire the cannon herself. That's the type of woman Cassie wanted to be, and every day brought her a new corporate battle in which she could fire figurative cannons. Whenever she was finished with a major project, she was exhausted—and so was everyone around her.

To the outside world, she had it all together—the right clothes, right car, right job. But her doctor knew she had something else: a stress-related ulcer.

Too bad she hadn't heard the statement from Helen Keller, the renowned American lecturer who was deaf and blind, "It's amazing what can be done when one person invites others to be part of the plan."

After the latest bout of severe stomach pain that required extensive medical tests, her doctor dropped the report onto Cassie's hospital bed. "I've known you for a long time," he said. "So I'm not going to beat around the bush. Whether or not you get well is in *your* hands, not mine. You have a choice: You can slow down by choice and learn to share responsibilities with your workforce or your body will force you to slow down through collapse. What will it be?"

He waited for Cassie's answer. Finally, she stammered, "But I'm the president *and* CEO of my company."

He remained unimpressed. Cassie narrowed her eyes as she added, "And the youngest of my group to be in such a position."

By now he had his prescription pad in hand. "It's up to you," he said as he handed her a slip of paper. "But it's tough to run a company from a hospital bed."

As he left, she glanced at his "prescription," which stated only, "Read the Book of Nehemiah. Don't try to build the wall alone."

Cassie gave an exasperated huff, then opened her

> *The thinking woman doesn't allow others to do her thinking for her. While she graciously listens to the counsel of others, ultimately she bases her choices on what she knows is God-pleasing and what she senses He is saying to her.*
>
> HELEN HOSIER

ever-present briefcase that was filled with books for those moments when she was stuck in traffic or when service was slow in the restaurant. There on the bottom of the stack was her Bible. She turned to the Book of Nehemiah and began reading, but soon sorted through her briefcase again—this time in search of a notepad and a pen.

Gather information, she wrote after reading of Nehemiah's questions to visitors about the Jews who had escaped exile and had remained in Jerusalem (1:2). Well, nothing new there. She never went into a new product line uninformed.

Pray. She paused as she read of Nehemiah's asking for God's direction (1:4). She knew she often jumped into a project without asking anybody's opinion—let alone God's.

Check feasibility of plan, she wrote next as she read of his requesting a leave of absence from his employer—the king (2:5-8).

Invite others to help. Suddenly she forgot about her list as she got caught up in the account of Nehemiah selecting those to accompany him to Jerusalem, where he methodically studied the ruins of the once-majestic wall. And always, he did everything only after he had prayed. Soon, the drama on the page was so real it was just as though she were watching it portrayed on a stage. In 2:17, she listened as Nehemiah invited the leaders and other citizens to be part of what God had directed him to do: "Then I said to them, 'You see the trouble we are in: Jerusalem lies in ruins, and its gates have been burned with fire. Come, let us rebuild the wall of Jerusalem, and we will no longer be in disgrace.'"

Let us *rebuild,* she read again. Then she felt a wash of relief. Maybe, just maybe, she could let the others in her business help, too.

Cassie was released from the hospital the next morning, armed with pills to tone down the stomach acid and her own determination to find other Scriptures that would help her run the business.

Soon, she had written the Lord's words of Matthew 11:28 in her notebook: "Come to me, all you who are weary and burdened, and I will give you rest." But in addition to His invitation for rest, He also reminded His followers of their dependence upon one another: Love one another (see Jn 13:34). Encourage one another (see Rom 15:2). Pray for each other (see Jas 5:16).

Cassie was beginning to understand that not only do we need others but that we have been created to be *inter*dependent rather than independent. But even as she inwardly agreed to that, she remembered a long-ago afternoon when she had called an uncle to ask his advice about a supplier. Instead of offering his opinion, though, he had scolded her, saying if she was going to run a business she'd have to figure out this stuff herself. That day, she had hung up, determined never again to ask for advice. Now she realized that maybe she'd caught him on a bad day, or maybe he didn't want to share in a few minutes what had taken him years to learn.

But what if she used that situation not as a directive to avoid asking for advice but as a reminder to pray before making a call? She thought about the old saying, "Pray as though everything depends on God and work as though everything depends on you."

She leaned back in her chair, then spoke aloud: "OK, Lord, please help me work on this area of my life. Show me ways I can be independent but still ask for help when I need to. I need Your help in this—and in every decision I face."

Boy, this is new stuff, she thought. *What if I make a mistake?* Suddenly she chuckled. *Well, mistakes aren't anything new. I won't always get it right, but as long as I pray first, and work hard and start inviting fresh ideas from others, I'll have less chance to fail, too.*

And with that thought, Cassie suddenly smiled. If she could actually put these new thoughts—and truths—into action, she knew her world was bound to be better—for her and for everyone around her.

Eight

I wish that you would want for nothing ... *and would be thankful for what you have.*

*G*od hasn't called me to be successful. He's called me to be faithful.

MOTHER TERESA

I recently ran into Debby, a young friend who was hired right out of college into a prominent business in the Midwest. As we chatted over mango tea, she sighed as she recited a long list of credit-card debt and confessed that her checking account was so horribly muddled she had been forced to change banks for the third time in order to open new accounts.

Even as I wondered how she—a bright woman of the new millennium—could have gotten herself into such debt, I could

sympathize with her checkbook agony. After all, I've gotten a lot of mileage out of my joke that the first time a friend asked if I had reconciled my checkbook after my husband died, I retorted, "Why do I have to reconcile myself to it? I'm not angry at it!" But financial ignorance is not funny—and financial disaster can result from a woman's decision not to manage wisely whatever amount she has.

Debby ended our mango tea discussion with the promise to accept the invitation from one of the bank officers to take their company's financial-planning class. As we parted, I felt confident she would get back not only financial but emotional freedom as well.

Another young friend, Jennifer, often meets with women from her church who either find themselves in financial trouble or who are having to make financial decisions alone for the first time. She always begins the session with a recounting of the afternoon she received her first allowance.

As she describes staring in delight at the two shiny quarters her mother had placed in her eight-year-old palm, you can almost see the sprinkling of freckles across the nose of that little girl. But along with the long-ago delight came the tougher lessons from her thrifty parent on how not to "waste" it. Jennifer caught on quickly to the concept that ten percent of the total should go to God in one form or another—either in the church offering plate or to missionaries of her choosing—not as a biblical command but as a way to say "thanks" for His many blessings.

Early on her parents had admonished her to set aside another ten percent in savings for a "rainy day." But Jennifer says she had trouble with this concept. After all, she had a long list of things she just had to have right *now.* Looking back today, she understands how it must have hurt her mother to tell her *no* when she asked for additional money for an outing with friends after she had blown the allowance for the latest fad. "But if my mother had bailed me out each time I wasted my money," Jennifer adds, "she would have taught me I didn't have to be responsible; that good old Mom would rescue me whenever I had any financial problems."

In one of her sessions with the women from her church, Jennifer grabbed her listeners' attention with the following thought: "Just as I learned to make financial decisions from my mother, your daughters will learn from you—for good or ill." This motivating thought has inspired many women to learn which bad habits got them into their troubled financial situation so they can learn how to get out.

Bad financial decisions often start when we make an impulsive purchase or give in to the lure of the latest fad. If you remember that fads change, and what is "in" today may look outdated tomorrow, then you will make wiser purchase choices. (If you aren't sure of the truth of that statement just ask your Aunt Jean about the avocado green and bright orange shag carpet she proudly displayed throughout her house in the mid-1970s.)

Secondly, we often spend money we don't have in order to impress people we don't like. That unidentified compulsion—and insecurity—may take us years to conquer, especially if we haven't grasped the truth of the Colossians 2:10 promise that we have "fullness in Christ."

While this Scripture is talking about spiritual fullness, we can readily apply it to material fullness, too. If we are aware of all we already have in Him, we aren't as prone to strive to fill our lives and hearts with more things. And that's all compulsive spending is trying to do—fill a hole in the heart. One way to test whether you're trying to fill an invisible emotional hole is to think of the times you've gone shopping only to return home with empty hands. Did you feel a little empty inside, too? If so, you're trying to fill a spot that will never be filled with just *things*. Even the richest man in the world was once asked by a reporter how much money is enough. "Just a little more," was the sad reply.

So if having all the money in the world is never enough if our hearts are empty, how do we make sound financial decisions with the money we do have?

First of all, don't make any financial decision without praying for guidance. I started to say, "Don't make any *major* purchase without prayer," but often it is the

Riches corrupt everybody who is in the least corruptible. God is merciful and can deliver the rich from the danger of being rich. But many of us act as though our trust is in riches.

<small>JOHN WHITE</small>

little seemingly unimportant purchases that ensnare us and trap us into impulsive buying. So go ahead and breathe a prayerful thought of *Should I buy this?* over even the little items. You'll find that the unspent dimes quickly add up to saved dollars.

For those big items—such as housing and cars—that we label as a legitimate need, *I have found that I make a better decision if I make it a regular habit to pray about the purchase for a minimum of three days.* And I've learned that if the salesperson is pressuring for an immediate decision, that's one business I'd better run from!

In all the financial decisions you face, remember that real security comes from the Lord—not from even the wisest of earthly investments. And even if we manage to gather great wealth, we are merely temporary stewards of His property.

Occasionally, you'll encounter people who believe it is too worldly to be concerned about financial matters, and they may even say money is evil. But 1 Timothy 6:10 says, "The *love* of money is the root of all evil" (KJV, emphasis added)—not money itself.

Money is inanimate; it's how it is used that matters. So the decision is yours: You can own your money or you can let your worry over money own you. But by choosing to follow sound financial principles, you will find a new freedom to concentrate on the truly important things that life offers.

Nine

**I wish for you a
compassionate heart ...
*that you may discern the
best way to help those
who need you.***

*Give to the
world the
best that you
have, and the
best will come
back to you.
Give Love, and
Love to your
heart will flow,
a strength in
your utmost
need.*

MADELINE BRIDGES

Catherine was a young English woman who at sixteen had an experience with God so vivid she said, "I was so happy that I felt as if I was walking on air." After marrying a young Methodist minister named William, she helped him lay the foundations for their work among the poor, first in London's East End and later throughout the country. In all she did, Catherine's ear was tuned to her Father for direction on who to help.

One day Catherine came upon a woman standing on a doorstep with a jug in her hand and despair written all over her face. Lots of

people had passed this woman by. Catherine had many responsibilities, and it would have been easy to rush past.

"Speak to that woman," the Lord whispered to her.

"But maybe she's intoxicated. Don't get involved," Satan said, in an attempt to derail her and stir up anxiety.

Catherine overcame her fears and offered the stranger help. She quickly discovered the woman's husband was a hopeless, abusive drunk. Catherine expressed her empathy and sorrow and then asked the woman if she could come inside.

"You couldn't do anything with my husband," said the woman. But Catherine wasn't dissuaded by the husband's drunken condition. Unafraid, she followed the woman inside.

The man was draped in a chair, jug in his hand. Catherine went to him, read him the story of the Prodigal Son and then earnestly prayed with him. Because of her small acts of kindness, the man turned to God, and his family's life began to be transformed. As Catherine continued in this kind of simple, faithful obedience to God and compassion to people, her example was a power for good that inspired many others to give themselves to the Lord's service. She and her husband William founded the Salvation Army, a ministry that goes on restoring the lives of the poor and needy to this day.[1]

Our self-centered world often turns a blind eye and

deaf ear to inconvenient needs. Yet, we are called to be Christ to those around us. My prayer for you is that you will find distinct ways to minister to those in your world, especially the hurting. May you

Do all the good you can,
By all the means you can,
In all the ways you can,
In all the places you can,
At all the times you can,
To all the people you can,
As long as even you can.

ANONYMOUS

never be too shy to offer what the Lord has given you and share what you know of His love. In doing so, you'll always want to be led by God's Spirit. Not to do the expedient thing, or give a token bit of help, but to give from the heart and minister as Jesus did.

As we see the enormity of human need around us, sometimes the very idea of responding seems like an exercise in futility. What we're doing seems like just a small drop in a huge ocean—it's not going to matter much.

But whatever good you do—whether it's praying for a hurting neighbor or one in need of God's healing presence, or tutoring a child who lives in a home full of turmoil, or giving to the poor or homeless in your community—know that what you do matters not only here but in eternity. The vast ocean would be diminished without your drop! What matters is not what a big thing you do, but that you do it out of love.

As Mother Teresa said, "God pays attention to our

love. We can work until we drop. We can work excessively. If what we do is not connected to love, however, our work is useless in God's eyes."[2]

Paul said it a long time ago in 1 Corinthians 13:

If I speak with human eloquence and angelic ecstasy but don't love, I'm nothing but the creaking of a rusty gate.

If I speak God's Word with power, revealing all his mysteries and making everything plain as day, and if I have faith that says to a mountain, "Jump," and it jumps, but I don't love, I'm nothing.

If I give everything I own to the poor and even go to the stake to be burned as a martyr, but I don't love, I've gotten nowhere. So, no matter what I say, what I believe, and what I do, I'm bankrupt without love.

1 CORINTHIANS 13:1-3, THE MESSAGE

How do we know if what we're doing is done in love? Paul explains:

Love never gives up.
Love cares more for others than for self.
Love doesn't want what it doesn't have.
Love doesn't strut,
Doesn't have a swelled head,
Doesn't force itself on others,
Isn't always "me first,"

Doesn't fly off the handle,
Doesn't keep score of the sins of others,
Doesn't revel when others grovel,
Takes pleasure in the flowering of truth,
Puts up with anything,
Trusts God always,
Always looks for the best,
Never looks back,
But keeps going to the end.

1 CORINTHIANS 13:4-7, THE MESSAGE

When we minister to others out of that kind of love, when we keep our ears tuned to God as to the best way to help those who need us; when we are sensitive and listen to their hearts, then our giving will preserve the dignity of the recipient and deliver a much-needed touch of grace.

1. Edith Deen, *Great Women of the Christian Faith* (Westwood, N.J.: Barbour and Company, 1959), 223–226.
2. Mother Teresa, *In My Own Words* (Liguori, Mo.: Liguori Publications, 1996), 39.

Ten

I wish for you security ...
*and an eternal
zest for life.*

Corrie ten Boom was born into a Christian family in Holland where her father owned and operated a watch shop. When World War II broke out in Europe and Hitler's forces were marching across Europe, their country came under Nazi occupation. Atrocities were being carried out against the Jews in their community by the Nazis, and hundreds were being sent to death camps.

Corrie's family had a tough decision to make—they could live for themselves and try to ensure their own safety, ignoring the plight of their Jewish neighbors, or they could

God is our refuge and strength, an ever-present help in trouble. Therefore we will not fear, though the earth give way and the mountains fall into the heart of the sea.

PSALM 46:1-2

risk their lives to protect them. The Ten Booms chose to put their own safety in God's hands and, in their three-story house, created a hiding place that housed Jews seeking refuge.

In time the activities of the Ten Booms were discovered, and the entire family was put in concentration camps. Even when her father had died and she personally was suffering, Corrie rose to her feet each morning and enthusiastically sang "Stand Up, Stand Up for Jesus!" She and Betsie, her sister, reached out to the devastated women around them in prison and gave them hope and encouraged them to put their trust in God. Corrie thanked God for little things, like the tiny parade of ants who brought her company when they marched through her cell. The sisters prayed for others and prayed for their own release from prison camp. Only Corrie survived.

Their story is dramatized in the best-selling book and movie *The Hiding Place*, which tells of the terror and suffering they experienced at the hands of the Nazis. You see, when Corrie got out of prison camp, although she was in her mid-fifties, she wanted to share her faith in God and her experience of His forgiveness and love with the world. So she began travelling from country to country, a "tramp for the Lord" as she called herself, speaking and ministering wherever she could, touching the lives of millions.

Although you probably won't be put in a situation as appalling as Corrie's, and though we aren't involved in the devastation of a war that comes right to our city or town, nevertheless, life is dangerous. The headlines of the past year attest to that fact as they catalog disasters and calamities—hurricanes, tornadoes, school shootings, plane crashes, urban violence and car wrecks. As Betsie ten Boom said, "The center of God's will is our only safety."

Realistically speaking, there are no guarantees—sometimes people fail us or tragedy or disappointments crash in upon our well-laid plans. We can choose to create our own "safe places"—emotionally, where we won't get so close to people or make commitments because they could hurt us or let us down; physically, where we take few risks and stay in a familiar, increasingly boring comfort zone in an attempt to build our own security; spiritually, where we are afraid of what God has in store, so we don't listen to His promptings and fail to follow His leading when it might be into uncharted territory.

The other choice is infinitely more interesting and full of potential: We can trust God, find our security in Him and face today and all our tomorrows with an eternal, enthusiastic zest for life. That is my wish, my prayer for you, dear one! That you'll choose the latter and abandon yourself to the One who made you and loves you even more than I do, and thus live full of excitement at what He has planned for you. That you'll trust God enough to answer a resounding *yes!* to His will and to life.

In fact, if there's a decision to be made and you're asking the Lord to show you the way to go, tell Him *yes* in advance, giving up any areas you're holding out, and joyfully committing yourself to God and what He chooses for your life even before you know where He's going to lead you.

Does this sound scary or difficult? Are you afraid if you say yes that God will send you to a remote place you always dreaded or put you in a job you hate? If so, that thought may come from the notion that He's a cruel killjoy waiting to spoil our fun. But the truth is "No eye has seen, no ear has heard, no mind has conceived what God has prepared for those who love him" (1 Cor 2:9). His will isn't a heavy or terrible thing—it's the greatest thing to discover in all of life.

Real Security

The Christian is guarded on all sides by the Lord:
We have God before us (see Is 48:17).
God behind us (see Is 30:21).
God on our right (see Ps 16:8).
God to our left (see Job 23:8-9).
God's loving arms uphold us (see Dt 33:27).
And protect us (see Ps 36:7).
His Spirit is within us (see 1 Cor 6:19).

As the above verses demonstrate, wherever we are and whatever may happen, God is with us and within us! With that kind of perspective, life becomes an adventure every day. In fact, Christianity *is the greatest adventure of a lifetime* when we walk with Him and do what He's planned. Listening and obeying. Listening and obeying. Day by day.

Sometimes, as in Corrie's experience, the steps God directs involve risk. In fact, someone said that *faith* is spelled "r-i-s-k." Taking those steps may lead you to a mission field across the world, as it did my friend Paula, who has served with her family in northern Thailand for almost twenty years. Following God's direction may lead you to a little school in Florida to teach migrant workers' children, to a publishing company in a big city, perhaps to a home and children of your own or a myriad of other destinies.

Psalm 119:105 says, "Your word is a lamp to my feet and a light for my path." It's a promise! When the Lord shows you a step to take and you take it, He'll give you just the light you need for your next step. As you live with an eternal yes to the Lord in your heart, you will never get bored. You will always have a future and a hope (see Jer 29:11). And He will always prove faithful. As George Mueller said, "Be assured, if you walk with Him and look to Him, and expect help from Him, He will never fail you."

**I wish for you
happiness …
*but not at the
expense of holiness.***

*Just as he who
called you is
holy, so be holy
in all you do;
for it is written:
"Be holy,
because I am
holy."*

1 PETER 1:15-16

That morning Kerri merely glanced at her reflection in the mirror as she splashed water onto her face. She had thought that going to bed with her new boyfriend would make her happy; she thought she'd wake up glowing and smiling the way the young career women in the movie scenes do. She had been the last of her group to keep her virginity; her friends were always kidding her about it. They thought that she needed to loosen up and live life the way it was supposed to be lived.

So last night, knowing her roommate would be out of town for the rest of the week with *her* boyfriend, Kerri had planned a romantic dinner, complete with candlelight and soft music. And after the raspberry torte, she had led her boyfriend to her bedroom, where he stayed until after midnight.

Now instead of smiling, she was trying not to look at herself in the mirror. She'd thought she'd be happy; she hadn't counted on this empty, lost feeling sitting in the pit of her stomach and the dread she had of running into *him* in the coffee room. This wasn't the way it was supposed to be at all. Suddenly she buried her face into the towel and sobbed, "I want to go back to the way I was!"

On the other side of town, another young woman, Linda, was dressing for her day as well—and smiling as she thought about meeting her old roommate for lunch. They'd catch up on personal news, then her former roomie would inquire about the guy in the shipping department and ask when she was going to go to bed with the "hunk."

Linda's coworkers didn't help matters with their accounts of their latest "conquests" or weekend trips with their boyfriends. But she'd seen the wistfulness in some of their faces when she said she was saving herself for her future husband. Often she even quoted to them the first part of Psalm 37:7—"Be still before the Lord and wait patiently for him...." Then within her mind, she would quote the rest of the verse: "do not fret when men succeed ..." *(or coworkers,* Linda thought) "... when they carry out their wicked schemes." This always helped her gain perspective after listening to their Monday morning "reports."

Linda understood that God wasn't being a killjoy when He set His guidelines, but that He wanted to offer something better than immediate and temporary solutions. Besides, He knows the human heart and understands the agony behind the

Whether it concerns her own or others' lives, the thinking Christian woman knows her thoughts, words and actions have eternal consequences. It is this knowledge that motivates her to evaluate all areas of her life in light of God's eternal values rather than the temporal ones of this world.

HELEN HOSIER

sad words "if only" and "oh, I wish."

In those moments when Linda was tempted to trade tomorrow's peace for today's gratification, she remembered the visual aid her ninth-grade biology teacher offered during the human-reproduction unit.

The teacher had called all the boys in the class forward to the front row, then handed the one closest to him a red, full rose with the instruction "Pull one petal and pass it on."

Bewildered, each boy plucked a beautiful petal and then passed the flower to his classmate. When the last petal was taken and only the stem remained, the

> *We belong to a Redeemer God, and it is never too late for Him to redeem anything!*
>
> EUGENIA PRICE

teacher had looked at the lad holding the barren rose and said, "That's your wife. Congratulations." Several of the students, boys as well as girls, had gasped.

Linda also had other thoughts that strengthen her in her fight against temptation: She understood that the problems came not from temptation but from how she chose to react to that temptation. *After all,* she reminded herself, *even the Lord Himself was tempted.* Hebrews 2:18 says, "Because he himself suffered when he was tempted, he is able to help those who are being tempted."

Since Jesus understood her struggles, Linda decided that the best thing she could do was to talk to Him about them and ask for continued strength, for godliness and for trust that the Lord would soon bring the right mate into her life. By inviting the Lord into every struggle, *especially* the sexual ones, she had a better chance to make good choices.

Prayer is the single greatest weapon against temptation we will ever possess. By admitting our dependence on God through prayer, we receive both the power to withstand temptation and God's peace as well. Prayer allows God to change difficult situations— or at least to change how we look at those situations.

While having lunch with a newly single friend one

day, Linda found that Donna was experiencing a dangerous attachment that psychologists call *transference.* Donna had been careful to guard against guys looking for one-night stands. Yet she found herself becoming dangerously attracted to her kind and helpful—and *married*—neighbor. She had never felt this kind of attraction before and wasn't sure how to handle it.

Because Linda had heard about transference, she was able to help her friend understand what was happening. All the energy and attention Donna had previously poured into marriage was now directed toward someone who was not an appropriate recipient.

Misunderstood transference can tempt lonely people into making inappropriate commitments or even into committing adultery. Linda had seen this happen once before, when another friend—the office "counselor"—had wanted to help a coworker who was having problems with his ex-girlfriend.

Her counseling "help" started with kind words, but then progressed to lunches and culminated in an affair that cost her church leadership and personal respect.

In the midst of that friend's grief, Linda gave her the long-admired embroidered wall hanging that had hung in her own office:

> *"Lord, I have a problem—it's me."*
> *"Child, I have an answer—it's Me."*

Over coffee the evening Linda presented the gift, the two young women talked about future decisions, settling on the tried-and-true concept of sublimation, which is nothing more than redirecting sexual energy into work, sports, creative productivity or other wholesome activities. Linda stressed that it is possible to live a fulfilled life without a present physical relationship. How?

1. By staying out of inappropriate dating situations.
2. By avoiding movies that will stir up longings.
3. By not reading inappropriate material.
4. By staying out of the "adult" corner of the video store.
5. By working hard and going to bed tired.

Linda had learned that by pouring her energy into other activities, she could remain genuinely fulfilled— and smile at herself in the mirror each morning.

Too bad Linda didn't know Kerri, the young woman who had sobbed that she wanted to go back to the way she was. If she had, she would have encouraged her with 1 John 1:9 which says, "If we confess our sins, he is faithful and just and will forgive us our sins and purify us from all unrighteousness."

We do not have to be bound by past decisions, nor are we doomed to repeat the same mistakes. No matter what has happened in the past, we can begin again to make good choices—starting today.

Twelve

**I wish for you
a heart of prayer ...
*and ears that hear
the Father's voice.***

*B*e still and
*know that
I am God.*

PSALM 46:10

Have you ever found yourself praying (or at least thinking) any of these prayers?

"Lord, help me relax about insignificant details beginning tomorrow at 10:32 A.M. EST...."

"God, give me patience, and I mean right *now....*"

"Lord, help me be less independent, and more dependent on You, but let me do it my way...."

"Lord, help me slow downandnotrushthroughwhatIdo!"

Prayer is simply intelligent, purposeful, devoted contact with God.

BRIGID E. HERMAN

Maybe, like me, you're something of a "Martha," our counterpart in the New Testament who was busy and distracted doing many things—so many things, in fact, that she didn't have time to sit at her Savior's feet. In fact, Martha seemed to resent her sister Mary's devoting herself to Jesus instead of helping her!

Like Martha, I have had *so many important things* to accomplish. During college it was studying and holding down a part-time job and spending time with friends. After I married it was the laundry, dishes, cooking, cleaning and trying to eke out time with my kids and husband. Prayer time at Jesus' feet?

But what Jesus spoke to Martha, He also meant for you and me: "You are anxious and troubled about many things; there is need of only one thing. Mary has chosen the good portion ... which shall not be taken away from her" (Lk 10:38-42, AMPLIFIED). That "one thing" is communing with our Savior and God through prayer.

One of the kindest invitations in the whole Bible, second only to salvation, is the invitation to cast all our cares upon the Lord, to pour out our heart to Him in prayer, because He cares for us affectionately and watchfully (see 1 Pt 5:7; Ps 62:5).

As women, we often go around carrying burdens

not only for ourselves, but for other people who are hurting, too: friends and coworkers, spouses and children. Those burdens get heavier and heavier if we carry them by ourselves. They dissolve our joy and even cause us to intervene when we should back off and control when we should let go, because we want so much to help.

Instead, God invites us to come to Him and have intimate conversation, to pour out those cares and burdens, all the contents of our heart, as if we were pouring out a pitcher of water at His feet, and then let our "pitcher" or heart be refilled with His love and hope before we rise and go on our way.

I love how Rosalind Rinker described prayer: "the expression of the human heart in conversation with God ... a dialogue between two persons who love each other."[1] Remember, a "dialogue" refers to *both* talking and listening. That means expressing all our needs, problems, feelings and emotions—holding nothing back, telling God what's truly in our hearts. Calling upon Him when we need wisdom, when we're afraid, when we need strength or courage. Making the Lord a part of all we do and think so that we begin to really know what it's like to "abide" in Him the way John talks about it: "Abide in Me, and I in you ... [she] who abides in Me and I in ... [her], bears much fruit; for without me you can do nothing" (Jn 15:4, 7, NKJV).

Yet prayer is not just our talking; there's the listening part of dialogue, since prayer's a conversation between *two people*, which means each wants to hear what the other person has to say. I don't know about you, but it's easy for me to do the talking and not allow God to get a word in edgewise. But God has so much to say to us. And with just a few words from His heart to ours, our lives can be changed.

I remember one of the significant times I distinctly heard God speak. Although I'd committed my life to Christ at age twelve, the loss of my father, several other family members and a close friend by age thirteen shattered my childlike faith and left me with many questions: *Does God care? Does He really hear my prayers? Are heaven and hell real, or was I just told about them to keep me from doing the wrong thing? Is the Bible true?*

After struggling with these questions throughout high school, my already fragile faith toppled when a professor in my freshman religion class informed us the stories of Noah, Creation and the Exodus from Egypt were merely myths. Outwardly, I went to church and kept up a good front, but inwardly my heart was growing darker and more discouraged. God and I weren't on close terms, much less carrying on an everyday conversation.

As I graduated from college and became a wife and mother, my search for meaning continued. One day, while my preschoolers napped, I was looking for something interesting to read. The last few years I'd spent my reading time studying British poetry and

The Spirit of prayer makes us so intimate with God that we scarcely pass through an experience before we speak to Him about it, either in supplication, in sighing, in pouring out our woes before Him, in fervent requests, or in thanksgiving and devotion.

O. HALLESBY

literature for a graduate degree, but now I searched the bookshelf and my hand hit upon an old Phillips translation of the New Testament. I picked it up and thumbed through it. Settling myself on the couch, I began to read all alone in the quiet room. I started with Matthew, read through Mark and then tackled Luke.

Day after day, page after page, as the boys napped in the afternoon I read just as I had so many textbooks the last few years. While reading the fourth book, John, several weeks later, I came across some very familiar words—in fact, I'd memorized them as a child: "At the beginning God expressed himself. That personal expression, that word, was with God and was God, and he existed with God from the beginning.... In him appeared life and this life was the light of mankind" (Jn 1:1-3, PHILLIPS).

As I read those words, I heard God whisper, "It's all true, every word." I really don't understand it, but as His words soaked in, it felt as if the whole room got lighter and warmer. And in the light of His love, years of doubts and skepticism melted away in that moment. In those five words, He addressed deep-down questions and turned the lights on in my spirit, beginning a life-changing renewal in my relationship with Him— and a dialogue between us that continues to this day.

Sometimes, as in this experience, God's whispers come through reading His Word, and other times He speaks to us through a glorious sunset or through a friend's words. We may hear Him through a chorus of birds singing, or recognize His still, small voice in our minds during devotional time or as we walk on a snow-covered road. And He loves to speak to us through the voice of a child. God speaks in times of joy, but most often it seems we pay attention and hear Him most clearly in times of anxiety or pain. "Pain," C.S. Lewis observed, "is God's megaphone to rouse a deaf world."

But one thing is sure: When God whispers from His heart to yours, when you hear Him and respond, something changes. Healing begins or an attitude is transformed. A relationship is restored or you're infused with hope and energy when you were just about out of steam. Sometimes His Spirit whispers vital direction for our job, relationships or ministry. And sometimes His whispers are meant to simply reassure us of His love.

He is *always listening.* When we pray and call out to Him, regardless of the time of day or night, He's attentive to our prayer, which means "straining His ears to hear"! And you don't have to have your life all cleaned up, figured out and fixed up for Him to attend to your prayer and send help. In fact, He's closest to those who have a broken heart, Psalm 34:18 tells us. God doesn't move away or change His number. He doesn't ask us to leave a message for later because He's too busy. The Lord is always home, and He loves to hear and speak to us.

My prayer and hope is that in every season of your life, no matter what responsibilities or tasks you have to do, you'll pour out your heart to God in a natural, honest conversation, and listen for His voice. Just as God spoke to His people in the Old and New Testament, He is speaking today, but sometimes the clattering culture around us drowns out His voice. Take time to get quiet and say, like Hannah's child of old, "Speak, Lord, Your servant is listening!" (see 1 Sm 3:10).

Take God up on His promise that if we call to Him, He will answer us and show us great and mighty things that we do not know (see Jer 33:3). *Ask* Him to speak to you! Then pay attention when He taps you on the shoulder in the middle of your commute or while you're at the computer or taking a walk. Take time to be still, stop striving, and know that He is God (see Ps 46:10). Read His love letters to you, the Bible, with a listening heart and keep tuned in to His Spirit all through the day. As you do listen and respond to the One who loves you the most, your life will be blessed beyond your dreams or imagination.

1. Rosalind Rinker, *Prayer: Conversing with God* (Grand Rapids, Mich.: Zondervan, 1959), 23.

Thirteen

I wish for you to know when to say "No" … *and when to say "Yes!"*

The wisdom of the prudent is to give thought to their ways, but the folly of fools is deception.

PROVERBS 14:8

Susan was everyone's friend and rescuer. If a friend needed someone to look after his dog while he was out of town, he called her. If a sister-in-law needed to practice her Monday-morning office presentation, she called Susan. If a nephew needed a tutor for Spanish class, he called Susan.

People around Susan were used to having their needs met through her. They were so used to it, in fact, that they resented her interest in a young assistant pastor who first asked her to dinner after they met while visiting a hospitalized mutual friend.

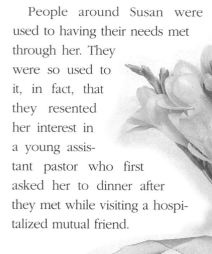

Another young woman, Amy, was drawn into every crisis her extended family experienced—whether it was the birth of new kittens or the breakup of yet another relationship. And each time the phone rang with another plea for help, she found herself getting more and more angry as she wondered, *Why do they insist* their *crises have to become mine?* That seething anger boiled out during a tense moment at the dress rehearsal for her niece's wedding. Yelling that she couldn't carry all of their burdens, Amy stormed out, demanding none of them were *ever* to call her again.

This area of knowing when to say *yes* and when to say *no* is a tough one. I don't want you to lose yourself in carrying everyone else's responsibilities. At the same time, I don't want you to be so self-absorbed that you refuse ever to move beyond your own comfort in order to help another.

Life will hand you plenty of moments when the only decent choice you can make is to stop everything you are doing to look to the well-being of a fellow traveller.

There will be times when you need to drop everything to help a panicked mother into your car so you can follow the ambulance to the emergency room. Or you may need to welcome the children of the young wife who is taking her husband for chemotherapy. Other times you will need to say to your fretting sister, "No, I'm sorry but I can't pick out new drapes with you."

A story is told of President Thomas Jefferson, who was travelling on horseback with his entourage, looking for a place to cross a rain-swollen river. At last they came to a narrow place that looked safe, between the two muddy banks.

As the group approached the water, a man stood up from under the tree where he had huddled for more than an hour. With rain dripping into his eyes, he looked into the face of each man. President Jefferson was near the end of the line, and it was to him that the man directed this question: "Please, sir, may I ride across the river behind you?"

The president nodded, then held his arm out so the man could swing up on his sturdy horse. As the group crossed safely to the other side, the man slid off the animal and thanked the president.

As the man started to walk away, one of President Jefferson's companions called to him. "Tell me, how is it you dared to ask to ride across the river behind the president of the United States?"

The man looked stricken. "Oh, I didn't know he was the president," he said to his accuser. "It's just that as all of you approached, I saw no in your faces and I saw yes in his."

There is only one way to find the balance between what you need to do and what you feel compelled to do. Ask the Lord for His help each day. Listen to His quiet instructions that often come through a fresh insight or new thought. And also listen to whether you groan at the opportunity to add one more activity to your day's to-do list.

Often when we complain about a busy schedule, that's our signal—no, our invitation—to start cutting a few projects.

You've heard numerous sermons about Martha in Luke 10—how she grumbled because the food preparation was left to her while her sister, Mary, calmly sat at the feet of Jesus, listening to His stories. As she stormed into the scene in Luke 10:41 and demanded the Lord send Mary to the kitchen to help her, He answered, "Martha, Martha, you are worried and upset about many things."

As a southern woman who grew up with the cooking philosophy of "Honey, I'd rather have a bushel too much as a teaspoon not enough," I understand Martha's fussing as she tried to prepare three meats, nine vegetables and at least two breads—one of which had to be Middle Eastern cornbread.

But Martha's problem was not in her *serving* the meal, but in her *attitude* toward serving. We know that to be true because we see her serving again in John 12:2, after her brother was raised from the dead—and this time without the Lord's reprimand. Apparently she took to heart His earlier words. Or perhaps losing her brother to death for even those four days put life into the proper perspective. Either way, she no longer was stomping around the kitchen, complaining that all of the work was on her shoulders.

As you try to discern the truly important from the merely frantic activities facing you each day, you may want to look at what I call the "John 5 Principle." It was the account of the healing at the pool that helped me get over my own worried-Martha hostess style. In the account of Jesus going to the pool located near Jerusalem's Sheep Gate, notice He went to *one* man to heal him. Now you let women like Martha—and me— loose in a scene like that, and we would feel as though we had failed unless every person there had been healed. But Jesus sees the man who had been paralyzed for thirty-eight years and asks him an important question in John 5:6: "Do you want to get well?" I find it interesting that the man didn't answer *yes* and he didn't answer *no*. Instead he said, in effect, "It's not my fault," as he said, "I have no one to help me into the pool when the water is stirred." How interesting that Jesus didn't argue with the paralyzed man—He wins *people* not arguments—but told him to take action: "Get up! Pick up your mat and walk" (v. 8).

Yes, sometimes Jesus will invite you to sit at His feet and listen to His quiet teachings. Other times He will give you specific instructions for action. And as you learn to listen to Him, you *will* know what action—or nonaction—you are to take.

**I wish for you
to love the Lord ...
*and to express
that love to others.***

*Decisions
must be
made in the
integrity of the
heart before
God—with an
unselfish atten-
tion to our
brother's good
and the glory of
God.*

ELISABETH ELLIOT

Nancy would have been con-
sidered by many to be just a
simple mountain woman, like
countless others who were raising
a family during the early part of
the twentieth century. But stories
of her faith in the Lord and compassion toward those she called
"pitiful souls" have affected several
generations.

During the Depression of the
1930s, when men roamed the
countryside looking for jobs
but settling for handouts,
Nancy often fed strangers
at her table, heaping
the bounty of her
country garden onto

the plates of despondent men who needed encouragement that the Lord had not forgotten them as much as they needed the food. Once she stepped into her garden just as a traveller hungrily bit into a plump tomato he had pulled from the vine. As Nancy watched the juice run down the man's chin, she quietly said, "You come on into the house. That'll taste better with the chicken and dumplings left over from dinner." The man gratefully followed.

Today, we don't have strangers showing up on our doorsteps asking for food—and, unfortunately, with the modern crime rate, we'd worry if we did—but we still have plenty of opportunities to encourage those around us.

I remember a tour I took years ago of Henry Ford's Greenfield Village, in Dearborn, Michigan. At Thomas Edison's laboratory, which is one of the sites transplanted from the East Coast, the guide showed us where the famous inventor had worked for thousands of hours to develop the incandescent light bulb. Finally the moment had come when he could present to the world the crystal containing the filament that could be heated by electric current, which in turn would produce the light that would push aside even middle-of-the-night darkness. Edison's staff assembled, holding their breaths with joyful anticipation as their boss handed the bulb to his assistant, who would attach it to the connecting stand.

Then the delighted, nervous assistant dropped it!

The rest of the staff gasped as they saw the crystal shatter. The assistant clutched his hands to his chest in numb horror. But Edison merely patted him on the shoulder and asked that another bulb be made. When that one was ready, the staff gathered a second time, with the embarrassed assistant standing back against the wall, far outside the gathering. But Edison glanced around, called him forward and then handed him the *second* bulb. What an incredible encouragement that gesture provided for the young man. And what an incredible example his compassion became for the rest of the staff.

Perhaps you won't choose inventions as your career, but life will still provide you with numerous opportunities to hand a "second bulb" to those who dropped it the first time. Plan *now* how you hope to react when a friend spills grape juice on your great-grandmother's tablecloth or when a child impulsively plucks the frosting roses off the cake you've decorated for the church banquet. Those moments *will* come. And long after the tablecloth has been cleaned and the frosting roses rebuilt, your reaction is what will be remembered.

We don't have to direct our kindness to only those folks we will see again. I remember a church trip that a friend I'll call Karen took with her two young children the summer after her husband died. The trip was

Kindness is the sunshine in which virtue grows.

ANONYMOUS

supposed to be a gentle respite in the midst of Karen's new status as a single mother, but frustration after frustration stormed into each day. Finally, the breaking point came, and as Karen stood with her children in the washroom line, she was close to tears. *How am I going to do this single-parent thing?* she wondered. *If today's tension was any indication of what's ahead, I might as well give up right now.*

Just then one of the grandmothers from the group walked past Karen. All day she had watched the young mother look around frantically for her son, who was prone to wander away, and trip over her daughter, who was so frightened by all of the strange sights that she clung to her mother's side. The grandmother spoke little English but as she patted Karen's arm, she said, "You *good* mama."

Suddenly, the young mother wasn't quite so exhausted, and her fears had been replaced with the hope that maybe, just maybe, she could pull this single-parenting thing off after all. And those three, simple words stayed in her mind—and heart—for years.

What I want you to understand is that making a difference in another person's life doesn't have to be dramatic. In fact, the greatest encouragement and the greatest statement of God's love often begins with our most simple gestures. And the simple practice of being *thankful* today can prepare us for tomorrow's challenges. So, starting today, make it a habit to surprise someone every day with a thank-you. You've told your friends about the teacher who encouraged you to make good choices, but have you ever told *her?* Even if you are convinced she won't remember you and certainly won't remember the situation, go ahead and send her a note. I suggest you write a note stating what she did or said that affected you, rather than calling, because I guarantee she will keep the note where she can read it again and again. We human beings need to know we have made a difference in the life of another, so your words will be carried in her heart forever.

Second, every day, thank God for something for which you have never before thanked Him. Have you ever thanked Him for your favorite color? I still remember the Colorado flower that caused me to exclaim my thankfulness for *purple*. And I remember the morning I thanked Him I could smell the *skunk* because that meant my sense of smell had returned after a long illness and that I would soon be able once again to enjoy the fragrance of the rose.

Finally, every day, thank God for something about which you are not now happy. For me, that often means I whisper, "Thank You that You are with me in this situation. Thank You for Your reality. Thank You that we do not pray to air." On those days when I'm struggling with yet another difficult situation, it helps me to remember that Philippians 4:4 says, "Rejoice in the *Lord* always" (emphasis added)—not in circumstances or in people.

As you grasp the reality of His presence, your new confidence in who He is will naturally spill into the actions you display toward those around you. What a difference that will make—not only in the lives of others but in your own life as well.

Fifteen

I wish for you to really like yourself ...
and to be proud of who God has made you.

The freedom to be one's self is better than carrying the burden of trying to be perfect.

KEITH MILLER

Renee leaned forward to better hear the psychology professor at the front of the lecture hall.

"Children learn early what the world thinks about them," he was saying, "and, in turn, the world's opinion shapes their own opinion about themselves. Believe me, there is no greater joy as a psychology clinician than to have a child smile as you ask her to say, 'I am a wonderful person.' Sadly, many children can't say that, and they grow into adults who feel as though they have no worth whatsoever."

Renee sat stunned, thinking, *How can anyone say, "I am a wonderful person"—especially a child?*

The professor glanced at his watch, then assigned chapter six for Monday's class before striding out. Renee slowly gathered her notes, wishing he had offered a solution, some "magic wand" counseling formula that would allow not only children but herself as well to say, "I *am* a worthwhile person."

As she walked to the library, Renee pondered the childhood events that had shaped her own opinion of herself. She had grown up knowing she was an "accident" that had altered her mother's education plans. Once, her mother had even snapped, "It's a good thing abortion wasn't readily available back then." How terrible to know your own mother would have killed you before birth if she'd had the chance. Oh, yeah, she knew about little kids not being able to say, "I am a wonderful person!"

She had hoped her Saturday-morning aerobics class would shake the ponderings out of her mind, but even with the psychology classes she had taken and her understanding that "hurting people hurt people," she still struggled with the invisible ropes tying her to an awful past.

Sunday morning, she idly flipped through radio stations, searching for something soothing. She stopped just as the deep voice of a local pastor said, "The family you came from is important, but not as important as the family you will leave behind."

Renee was stunned and barely heard the rest of his comments. She certainly didn't want to pass on to her future children the baggage she had carried throughout her own youth, so several days later, she called the church. That afternoon, she was sitting in the pastor's office, stammering her reason for being there.

"I'm tired of carrying all this junk around," she said. "I'm tired of feeling worthless. I'm tired of not getting anyplace in life. I'm tired of not feeling really loved." Then she shrugged and added, "But, hey, I don't like myself, so how can I blame anybody else for not liking me, either?"

The pastor nodded. "Are you familiar with the Alcoholics Anonymous phrase 'sick and tired of being sick and tired'? That's just what you've described. And that's good because it means you're ready for a change. First, you need to understand that you *are* loved already. Listen to what Romans 5:8 says: 'But God demonstrates his own love for us in this: While we were still sinners, Christ died for us.'

"But you don't understand," she said. "I've made some pretty stupid choices. And every night those stupid choices perch at the head of my bed, ready to attach themselves to me the next morning. Every time I get a little hopeful about stuff, I figure *why bother?*"

The pastor leaned forward. "When we concentrate on our failings instead of the Lord's power and grace to free us from the guilt of having failed, we're helping Satan. After all, as long as we're beating ourselves up, he doesn't have to!"

He picked up a marker pen and drew three

interlocking circles with a stick figure inside.

"You can see I'm not much of an artist," he said, "but the trapped figure is you, and these circles represent the three different types of guilt: true, false and misplaced."

Renee stared at the paper as he continued. "True guilt is when you have done something wrong and the only way you can get rid of that nagging dread is to confess it to God and accept His forgiveness. Sometimes that means you have to say, 'I'm so sorry, will you forgive me?' to somebody else, first."

Sudden tears sprang into Renee's eyes as she thought of the argument she'd had with her thrifty grandfather over the purchase of a new lawn mower he had wanted and could afford, but had refused to buy. She had called him a "stupid old man," and he had retorted in kind by calling her entire generation "leeches who demand everything right now." She had stormed out of the house and didn't contact him again. Four months later, a cousin called with the news their grandfather had died of a sudden heart attack. Instead of going to the funeral home, Renee had gone out partying with a group from her psychology lab.

Now in the pastor's office, Renee stared at her broken thumbnail and whispered, "Yeah, but what if you can't tell them you're sorry. What if they're dead?"

The pastor's expression softened. "Some counselors suggest you write them a letter you don't mail or you talk to an empty chair you pretend they're sitting in. But for those times I've needed to ask forgiveness when it's too late to talk to the person, I just pray—usually crying a little bit—and ask the Lord to tell them I'm sorry."

He paused, then said, "Would you like to do that now?"

Renee shook her head. "No, I gotta think about that some more. But I'd like to hear about the other two guilts."

The pastor turned back to the paper. "The other two—false and misplaced—are mean because they come in so handy when we want to help Satan beat us up.

"With false guilt you are convinced everything bad is your fault, and you'll use a lot of 'I should haves' when you talk about the situation, such as even blaming yourself for your friend's accident when it was caused by a drunk driver who ran the stop sign."

Renee stared at the circle, trying to fit his words into the guilt she had carried over her mother's decision to leave college those years before.

The pastor tapped the third circle. "With misplaced guilt, you have something happening that normally would be insignificant, but this time it causes a deep problem. It can be something as simple as thinking that it's your fault a friend didn't do well in a game because you—the designated laundry doer—threw her 'lucky' socks in the wash."

"So where do I start?" Renee asked. "I'd love it if you have a magic-wand formula."

The pastor smiled. "I don't have a magic wand, but the old teacher in me does have several assignments.

"First, starting today, I want you to ponder how much God loves you. He loves you so much that, as it says in John 3:16, He sent His own Son to die for our sins—yours and mine. For the whole world's, in fact.

"Then, start coming to church. We have a large college and career class, and you need to hang around kids your age who are willing to talk about these issues. They've been there, too.

"Next, I want you to find ways to add more laughter in your life. Proverbs 17:22 says, 'A cheerful heart is good medicine, but a crushed spirit dries up the bones.' Laughter will help open your crushed spirit to God's healing. If you don't know where to start, rent movies from the classic comedies section at the video store. My favorites are the Marx Brothers.

"And finally, find a way to serve others. I guarantee that as you make a difference in the life of another, you'll find greater joy in your own. Fair enough?"

Renee nodded. "Fair enough," then thought, *I'm on my way to being a worthwhile person after all.* And suddenly she smiled.

Sixteen

I wish for you a way to express yourself …
to reflect the unique creation God intended you to be.

What you are is God's gift to you.
What you make of yourself is your gift to God.

ANONYMOUS

One of the most exciting things I've discovered is the different ways God has "wired" each of His creations. There's nothing happenstance or random about how He has designed each person, including you! God had something special in mind when He gave some people visual, artistic talent and others perfect pitch and the ability to compose music; when He gifted some with verbal communication skills, gave leadership talent to other people and gifts of mercy and compassion to some.

And He had something special in mind when He made *you.*

After all, the Lord had songs He wanted to be sung, organizations He needed to be started and managed. There were books and messages thought of in heaven He needed hands on earth to write. He wanted stained-glass windows created to give us a glimpse of glory as the sun shines through, marvelous paintings and colorful gardens to fill our world with beauty and reflect His love. So He gave gifts to men and women to accomplish these and many other of His purposes. As James 1:17-18 says, "Every good and perfect gift is from above, coming down from the Father of the heavenly lights, who does not change like shifting shadows. He chose to give us birth through the word of truth, that we might be a kind of firstfruits of all he created."

I was reminded of this unique designing of individuals when I worked in a summer arts camp for gifted junior high students one summer. As a writer, I worked with the verbally talented kids as they created poems and stories. A musician directed the vocalists and those who played instruments, and a drama coach worked with the star-struck thespians. But perhaps most interesting to me was the dance teacher, a ballet choreographer. At the end of the week, she and the dancers made up graceful movements and dance steps to interpret the poetry that was created and read by my students.

As I watched Maggie choreograph and dance, I was

struck by the fluid grace and originality of movement. When I commented on this, she said—as if we all shared this kind of talent—"Oh, I just think in movement all the time. That's just how my mind works. When I hear music or poetry, I see dance steps and a whole flow of movement in my mind." To me—someone who thinks primarily in words, not movement or pictures—this was an amazing talent.

My friend Marsha, who is a ceramics and pottery artist, can look at a lump of red clay and see a porcelain angel—and then create a whimsical, colorful one in an afternoon. Kay, the student ministries director at our church, has terrific ability at leading and teaching college students to become dynamic house-church pastors on their university campuses and at taking them on life-changing mission trips. My sister Marilyn is thrilled by anything about science and teaches chemistry and biology to high-school students through exciting experiments. And my sister-in-law Lou Ann has the analytical, math and administrative talent to create a financial plan for an entire city. Annick Goutal, the celebrated French perfumer, is an artist, but fragrances are her canvas. She composes her fragrances much the way a musician creates his music. Some of her famous fragrances she dreamed of in her sleep, or were an expression of her most deeply felt emotions and memories. To Annick, perfume is the music of the senses, and she is wired to create timeless combinations of spices, fruits and flowers.

We must first see the vision in order to realize it; we must have the ideal or we cannot approach it. But when once the dream is dreamed, it is time to wake up and get busy. We must do great deeds, not dream them all day long.

LAURA INGALLS WILDER

Just as He has with each of these women, God has uniquely designed *you* with gifts and talents—and He has wonderful, and sometimes surprising, plans for how He wants you to use them. My heartfelt hope is that you'll discover those gifts within and utilize them as a way of expressing who you are and what you think and dream—but also as a way of blessing others and glorifying God. Because I believe since that creative spark within you is a reflection of His creative Spirit, when you exercise it by using your gifts, you will experience an irrepressible joy—the same kind of joy Olympic runner Eric Liddell spoke of when he said, "God made me fast; and when I run, I feel His pleasure," in the movie *Chariots of Fire*. When you are using the gifts God gave you, you'll find yourself operating in a maximum of effectiveness and a minimum of weariness because you are doing what He made you for.

The same Spirit inspired the gifts of leading and motivating people, art talent, writing poetry or fiction, the ability to make money, creative ability in any field, organization and administration, people skills, gifts of mercy, teaching and encouragement, musical talent and all the others I could name.

How can you discover and develop these gifts and experience this kind of joy? The first place to start is giving yourself—body, soul and spirit—to God in the way that Romans 12:1-3, THE MESSAGE (emphasis added), suggests:

> Take your everyday, ordinary life—your sleeping, eating, going-to-work, and walking-around life— and place it before God as an offering. Embracing what God does for you is the best thing you can do for him. Don't become so well-adjusted to your culture that you fit into it without even thinking. Instead, fix your attention on God. You'll be changed from the inside out. Readily recognize what he wants from you, and quickly respond to it. Unlike the culture around you, always dragging you down to its level of immaturity, *God brings the best out of you,* develops well-formed maturity in you.

As you present yourself as a living vessel to the Lord, day after day, and invite Him to live through you, you'll find your true self—and discover your unique gifts. The more you know Christ, the more you'll be at home with how He's made you.

Having done that, the same twelfth chapter of

Romans has the next step for utilizing your gifts:

Go ahead and be what we were made to be, without enviously or pridefully comparing ourselves with each other, or trying to be something we aren't.

If you preach, just preach God's Message, nothing else; if you help, just help, don't take over.... If you give encouraging guidance, be careful that you don't get bossy; if you're put in charge, don't manipulate; if you're called to give aid to people in distress, keep your eyes open and be quick to respond; if you work with the disadvantaged, don't let yourself get irritated with them or depressed by them. Keep a smile on your face.

ROMANS 12:3-8, THE MESSAGE

Seventeen

**I wish for you
to be able to
tell the truth ...
*and to hear it gracefully.***

*It is not
because
things are good,
but because He
is good that we
are to thank the
Lord.*

HANNAH
WHITALL SMITH

Michelle plopped the lamb chops into the skillet to brown, then halved the fresh apricots and hastily chopped the onions—glancing at the clock all the while. Charles would be here in an hour. Sighing, she wished she hadn't promised to make this complicated dish tonight, but he always raved when she served curried lamb and apricots. His job kept him on the road—and in restaurants—much of the time, so when he was in town she didn't want to disappoint him.

She smiled, remembering how she had pored over her cookbooks for several days before

that first dinner, then settled on the exotic-sounding dish. That night, she had watched Charles closely as he took the first bite. How relieved she had been when he said, "This is really good. Really. In fact, these are the best chops I've ever had."

Even with today's long meeting at work, she wanted Charles to understand that he was important to her— important enough to fuss over. Besides, she was convinced he was working up to the Big Question, and she wanted nothing to stand in the way.

She sautéed the onions in butter, then added the flour, salt, milk and curry, stirring all the while. As the sauce began to bubble, she added the mushrooms, then poured the mixture over the chops and apricot halves she had arranged in a baking dish.

There! Now to toss the salad while the chops baked. Good thing she had set the table last evening after Charles had called to confirm tonight's date. But, of course, that was so much like him. *He truly is the nicest guy in the world,* she thought. *And worth every minute I have to spend on this dish.* Just as the oven timer went off, the doorbell rang.

The evening went just as Michelle had envisioned— even to the stroll onto her patio to look at the city lights against the foothills of the Rockies. After a long moment, Charles took a deep breath, then dropped to one knee.

Looking up at her, he said, "Michelle, surely you know I love you. When I'm on the road now, I can't wait to come home—because of you. Will you marry me?"

Tears welled in her eyes at his words and the sweet, old-fashioned gesture of him on his knees.

"Oh, Charles, yes," she said. "Of course, I'll marry you."

He stood up to put his arms around her as he murmured, "Oh, thank you!"

She expected him to kiss her then, but instead he stammered, "Since we're gonna be married, I've got to tell you this: Please don't fix curried chops *ever again.* I can't stand curry."

Michelle pulled back to look at him, stunned. Why hadn't he told her before? Why had he let her continue to prepare a dish he hated? Then her mind raced. How would he face the challenges of marriage if he had let her believe a *lie* for all these months?

Poor Michelle. Poor Charles. Was he really being dishonest? Or had he thought it kinder to spare her immediate feelings only to get caught in a further complication? Was he afraid of Michelle's response to the truth—that she would, in fact, reject him if he rejected her curried chops? In another person, this scenario might have revealed a character flaw, but in the case of Charles, it was his determination not to hurt Michelle's feelings that had created the tangled situation. But Michelle felt only dismay—and not appreciation—for his choice.

Psalm 119:30 is a great guideline for life—even for

Every moment of our lives we are faced with spiritual hazards, and at the same time with spiritual opportunities.

ELISABETH ELLIOT

decisions such as the one Charles faced that first evening when the curry hit his tongue: "I have chosen the way of truth; I have set my heart on your laws." So, if he had followed that principle and then added the Ephesians 4:15 admonishment to speak the truth in love, he could have said, "This dish is well prepared and tasty, but curry isn't my favorite spice."

Not only would Michelle never again have prepared that particular dish, but the remark would have allowed her to ask what spices he did like—and, thus, get to know him even more. Yes, his honest response would have hurt her feelings a bit but only for a little while. And how much better to do that than to prolong—and deepen—the hurt.

One caution: Notice that the truth is to be spoken "in love." Too often someone wants to cloak meanness under the title of "truthfulness"—as when Jill told her sister that the lavender dress made her look *even fatter.* To speak in love also means that you offer at least two compliments for every criticism—as when Charles could have first said that the dish was well prepared and tasty, even though he didn't care for the spice itself.

The Scriptures are filled with examples of the importance of telling the truth—such as 1 Samuel 1:1-17. In this account, Hannah had no children—unlike her husband's other wife, Peninnah. One year, during the annual trek to the temple, Hannah, in anguish, moved her lips as she prayed silently, asking for a child. The priest, Eli, misunderstood and wrongly accused her of being drunk. When Eli accused her of drunkenness, Hannah had several choices. She could lash out at him in anger; she could tearfully slip away, crying about being wrongly accused; or she could choose a third— and correct—response: communicate directly and respectfully with her accuser. She chose the latter.

To Eli's accusation, Hannah replied, "Not so, my lord ... I am a woman who is deeply troubled. I have not been drinking wine or beer; I was pouring out my soul to the Lord" (v. 15). Eli then said, "Go in peace, and may the God of Israel grant you what you have asked of him" (v. 17). By the next year, Hannah became the mother of Samuel, a future godly priest.

And while it is important to lovingly *tell* the truth, it is equally important to *hear* the truth. The following suggestions will help you better deal with any criticism, and help you choose which comments to accept and which to discard:

1. Listen to the criticism all the way through. Don't try to argue in the middle of it since it puts you into a defensive position and won't allow you to hear anything that may be helpful.

2. Understand that not all criticism is accurate. To help you decide, listen for those comments that ring true

within your own spirit as they verbalize what you have known, but had trouble putting into words.

3. It helps if you can take notes while another is offering criticism. Jotting down both the bothersome and the helpful phrases allows you to ask questions about specific points without interrupting.

4. Take the criticism at face value. Try not to bring old childhood issues—such as abandonment or fear—into this situation.

5. Apply what you find useful, discard wrong perceptions and get on with life. To wallow in any self-pitying feelings created by the criticism is defeating.

6. Bring a sense of humor to every criticism. When I taught the classical myth of Helen of Troy, whose face launched a thousand ships, one student asked, "Does it bum you out to talk about her, since your face wouldn't launch a rowboat?" I chose to laugh then rather than scold him. A grumpy response would have created a scene—and further challenges. By laughing at his barbed wit, I disarmed him—thus, eliminating future verbal battles—and I won a new friend in that student. He, along with the others, remembered my *reaction* long after they had forgotten his jab.

And while Michelle and Charles learn from their experience, may they someday be able to laugh at it as well.

Eighteen

I wish for you an active, energetic lifestyle … *now and for the rest of your life.*

Finding the time and making your workout the priority in taking care of yourself will determine whether you win for the long run. It's a life-giving process.

OPRAH WINFREY

Anne-Marie, a young woman I knew in college, never had to worry about her weight—until her freshman year at the university. Then because of eating the high-fat food in the dorm cafeteria and dividing her time between studying, a part-time job and dating (mostly sitting-down activities), Anne-Marie found herself almost ten pounds heavier than she'd ever been. It was no consolation that people said, "Oh, that's just the Freshman 10—everybody packs it on!"

After returning to school and bemoaning her new "weight problem," she and her roommate Jen (who'd

also put on weight) began to brainstorm and came up with their own rescue program for their bodies: For the spring semester, they would eat only half their food at breakfast, lunch and dinner. Not skipping meals, but cutting down on quantity. And to increase their activity level, they'd both dust off their tennis rackets, start practicing regularly and sign up for the intramural tennis program.

With some effort and encouragement, the two coeds stuck with their resolve and were both back to their ideal weights and filled with energy to spare by spring break.

"It's not where you start but where you finish that counts," says my friend Shari Shepherd. So many people start in a bad place and feel like they're stuck there. Shari knows, because as a teenager she made a lot of poor choices—from the kids she hung out with to the junk food she ate. She was overweight and her physical condition was getting worse. By age sixteen Sheri was sixty-five pounds overweight and miserable.

Finally she listened to her stepmother's advice and turned to the Lord for help. She made some positive changes and began exercising and eating healthy for the right reasons—to honor God with her body. She eventually began to share what she learned with other women and produced a fitness video and book called *Fit for Excellence* that's inspired hundreds of people to make better choices about their health.

Does it surprise you that this whole topic of exercise

would be so important that it would be one of my fondest wishes for you? This hope—that you'll always make exercise a vital part of your lifestyle—may sound a little unspiritual to you or even selfish. Recently on Christian radio I heard a caller say she thought it seemed selfish to use our time for workout or exercise when we should be out doing evangelism or ministering to someone. But the truth is you won't have the energy and enthusiasm to do and be all God plans if you don't take care of the body He gave you.

The Lord made you spirit, soul *and body*. Psalm 139 tells us He took special care with creating every part of your physical body. He breathed His very life into you. He uniquely designed you, from your head and hair color (which most of us ladies love to highlight or change and I think must make God chuckle—"I thought she'd love that red or brown, curly or straight hair I designed—there she goes changing it again!") right down to your toes.

"You made all the delicate, inner parts of my body, and knit them together in my mother's womb. Thank you for making me so wonderfully complex! It is amazing to think about. Your workmanship is marvelous—and how well I know it" (Ps 139:13-14, LB).

Now, just like all the other gifts He has given you, God wants you to be a good steward of your body. To respect it, treat it kindly, feed it the healthy foods it needs to thrive—and to move it regularly.

When you were a preschooler, like most kids you

were like an Energizer bunny moving, playing, jumping, dancing spontaneously. We didn't have to worry about your getting enough exercise. But every year, most kids become a little more sedentary until, by the teenage years, about a third of young people are inactive and well on their way to becoming ardent couch potatoes. And many of them are overweight.

Let's take a look ahead to what happens if you proceed on the path of inactivity through your twenties and thirties. I know it seems like a *long* way in the future, but it'll be here before you know it! If you're like most women, your metabolism will start slowing down in mid-life, and keeping fit then can be as difficult as swimming upstream—especially if you've spent several inactive years or haven't gotten into the habit of exercising.

So let me encourage you—start now! Move your body! Not just while you're young, but for your whole life. Exercise. Turn up the CD player and dance. Take strolls around your neighborhood. Bike around the lake with a friend. Jump for joy! As you do, you'll find the benefits of an active lifestyle are many: You'll have more energy. You'll be more optimistic and handle the stresses of life with more ease. You'll have a lot more fun, live longer and be stronger.

How can I make the time? you may be wondering. It's easy to get so busy with your job, ministry, responsibilities, demands and needs of family and friends that you neglect your own health to the point that the only walking you do consists of dragging from the bedroom to the kitchen for coffee. Then a few steps to the car that takes you to work, then back to your car eight hours later and parking your body in front of the TV for the evening.

If that's the sum total of your daily exercise, dear one, you'll be likely to join the millions of Americans who are overweight (recent statistics say half of all Americans are tipping the scales much higher than we should for good health). If you're flabby and unfit, you won't have the energy to tackle the challenges of a career or of parenting and juggling all the roles we women do. You'll likely feel fatigued and look to another cup of coffee to put some spring in your step. And you may not feel excited when God has another responsibility or another "mountain" of difficulty for you to climb, because you're just too tired. It's hard to mount up with wings and soar like an eagle when you're plagued by exhaustion!

You see, we get more energy by exercising (it's kind of like having a bank account that we make deposits in—the more you deposit by moving your body, the more zest and energy you'll be able to draw out). And because daily exercise speeds up metabolism so your body can better burn the calories you consume, a side benefit is weight control. As Denise Austin, fitness expert, says, "Exercise regularly and you will control your weight for life."

In addition, when you take time to renew your

Do you not know that your body is the temple (the very sanctuary) of the Holy Spirit Who lives within you, Whom you have received (as a Gift) from God? You are not your own, you were bought with a price (purchased with a preciousness and paid for, made His own). So then, honor God and bring glory to Him in your body.

1 CORINTHIANS 6:19-20, AMPLIFIED

energy each day by exercise—walking, strength-training workouts at the gym, rollerblading, if that's your favorite, playing softball with the church or company team or tennis with a friend—you'll be amazed at your growing sense of well-being, the way you can better handle everyday stress, the stamina you have and even more buoyant, optimistic moods.

Why? Endorphins—hormones that act much like an "upper," only are quite natural—are released when you exercise, warding off depression and boosting sagging spirits. At the same time, unneeded adrenaline is released from your body tissue when you exercise aerobically, thus relieving the body of some of the stress it carries. What this adds up to is living a longer, healthier, more vibrant and enjoyable life.

Just a hint—find an activity *you* really *enjoy* and one that is so much fun you look forward to it. Then you'll find it easier to stick with over the long haul. Your best friend may love the StairMaster, but if you don't, you'll put off workouts. A kickboxing class set to lively music may be more your style. You may be a solitary exerciser, enjoying the time to jog and talk to God at the same time. Or you may be a more social exerciser who likes to do something active with people. In that case, find a walking partner or attend an aerobics class with other women. Find what works for you—that may be a single activity or a combination of activities—do it at least three times a week, and then stick with it!

Do it not to glorify yourself for the wrong reasons, to have a perfect body you can flaunt, but eat and exercise to glorify God with your body and to have the energy to do all He's called you to do as a college student or wife or mother or in full-time ministry or the workplace. You'll be so glad you did!

Nineteen

I wish for you to see the best in others ... *without being blind to their weaknesses.*

> *Going to church doesn't make you a Christian any more than going to a garage makes you an automobile.*
>
> BILLY SUNDAY

Diane was thrilled the well-known author and speaker, whom I'll call Mrs. Miracle Worker, had hired her as an assistant. Her job included travel arrangements, baggage handling, ice fetching, clothes pressing and any other details Miracle tossed her way.

Before each platform appearance, Diane would slice a fresh lemon into thirty-two precise slices for munching or dropping into ice water. Then during the presentation, she would sit to the side, armed with a yellow pad

for the to-do list Miracle would toss at her on their way back to the hotel. Diane had learned to take notes quickly; an irritated Miracle would snap instructions if she had to repeat anything.

About two months into the assignment, Miracle actually had screamed at Diane for not packing the *backup* cell phone, even though it hadn't been needed on the trip they were just finishing. Diane had apologized and even cried, promising to check her list more carefully the next time. *I'm so stupid* was the thought that kept running through her head for several days. Then Diane witnessed something the following weekend that let her know she wasn't the one with the problem.

At a Florida conference, a timid-looking woman approached Miracle in the ballroom lobby.

"I must tell you how much I admire your Bible teaching," she managed. "In fact, I have every one of your books."

Miracle smiled. "Every one? Why, there are five books in the first series alone."

The woman nodded. "And seven in the second series."

Miracle glanced at her watch. "Yes, and my latest book is available at my booth. Do buy it, and I'll autograph it for you. Well, I must run."

The timid woman took a deep breath to gather all her courage and said, "May I hug you before I go?"

Miracle looked appalled. "Oh, I'd rather you didn't,"

she said. "My makeup and hair are just so, and I don't want to be mussed up."

The timid woman's face flushed as she nodded and quickly turned away. Diane felt embarrassed and heartsick. Her long-admired mentor, the one she held up as an example of the Perfect Christian Woman, had proven herself to be just another stage performer.

Diane noticed that the woman did not stop by the booth after the presentation. The next morning, Diane saw her checking out of the hotel even though the conference would continue another two days. She wondered what the woman would do with all of Miracle's books once she arrived home. Probably nothing. She would just make sure she never again asked for something as "intimate" as a public hug.

That evening, when Diane tried to talk to Miracle about the scene, she was met with bewilderment. Miracle didn't understand why "fans"—as Miracle called the women in her audiences—were always wanting to hug her. With a wave of her hand, she let her young assistant know the discussion was ended.

Yes, it would have been wonderful if Miracle hadn't worried about an adoring "fan" mussing her hair or smudging her makeup. But how nice, too, if the admiring woman hadn't expected so much from just another human being.

Diane was learning the hard way that people, no matter what their position, are just *people*. And in her close work with Miracle, she learned that whenever

> *God has always used ordinary people to carry out His extraordinary mission.*
>
> CAROL KENT

she set her hopes too much on another person, sooner or later, she was bound to be *disappointed*. And judging from the way she had let her own devotional life slide lately, she knew she was heading toward *discouragement,* which could quickly propel her into *disheartenment.* She suddenly understood the accounts she had heard of others leaving not only public ministry but even the church.

Now she had a choice to make: She could resign her position as assistant to Mrs. Miracle Worker. Or she could just take a deep breath and continue in this role but without the gushy adoration. After much prayer and a return to her own study of the Word, she chose to stay only for another two months. Then to her great delight, she found a position with another author, whom I'll call Peace, who lived her faith each day—and who taught the young woman what it means to listen to the Lord even in the midst of an intense schedule.

One of the lessons Diane learned from her new boss was the truth of Romans 15:1-2: "We who are strong ought to bear with the failings of the weak and not to please ourselves. Each of us should please his neighbor for his good, to build him up."

As she watched her employer encourage the other members of the speaking team, she saw the truth of the Lord's words in John 13:34-35 lived out: "A new command I give you: Love one another. As I have loved you, so you must love one another.... All men will know that you are my disciples, if you love one another."

This woman had a gentle way of encouraging the other members of her staff as she publicly pointed out their strengths and privately suggested areas they might want to think about changing. One serene afternoon, as Diane and her employer, Peace, checked the travel itinerary for the next week, Diane timidly thanked her for never yelling, then asked her how she managed to bring out so much good in her staff.

Peace smiled. "Oh, I do plenty of yelling," she said. "I just reserve that for the neighborhood dogs who dig in my flower garden and not for fellow travellers in this thing we loosely call 'life.' You see, the Lord taught me a long time ago that if He could love and use Peter even though He knew the salty old fisherman was going to deny Him publicly three times, then who am I to judge how folks are going to turn out."

Peace put on her glasses, then reached for her ever-present Bible and turned to John 13:38. "This is just one of the Gospel accounts of Jesus predicting that the very man who had just said he would lay down his life for the Lord would, in fact, deny Him three times before daybreak." She read the verse and then added, "And by John 18:27, that's exactly what happened."

Her employer flipped through several more pages.

"Now look in Acts 2:14." She continued, "Here Peter is preaching at Pentecost." Peace turned the page. "And in verse 41, it says that about three thousand souls became believers that day. Even more followed that number—and through the preaching of the very one who had denied the Lord *three* times."

Peace again smiled at Diane. "To see the best in others without being blind to their weaknesses is an example our Lord set numerous times. And as long as we keep our eyes on Him and off ourselves, miracles will continue to happen—first in us and then in the folks around us."

As her employer took off her glasses, Diane made a mental note to read the account for herself that evening. So *this* was what it meant to be a follower of the Lord.

**I wish for you not
to put off joy …
*but to celebrate life today
and every day.***

*For the heart
that finds joy
in small things,
in all things
each day is
a wonderful gift.*

UNKNOWN

My one-time neighbor Sally was an idealist and had high expectations about how her life was supposed to be going. She had four wildly energetic kids; twenty pounds she'd gained during her pregnancies, weight she desperately wanted to get rid of; and a husband who worked so many hours he was rarely at home.

"When I lose this weight, then I'll be happier," she'd tell me over our tuna sandwiches at the park as we chatted under a shade tree while our children raced around playing. "When John starts coming home on time, then I'll fix nice dinners," she said. "And when these kids grow up and stop being so messy and the broken cabinets get fixed, I'll wallpaper and start keeping the house cleaner!" Unfortunately, as long as I knew Sally, things never got good enough and she kept putting off joy until some far-off day when all would be right.

If, like Sally, you're always thinking you'll experience the joy you want when you lose that weight or when you land that wonderful job you've been interviewing for or your child starts making better grades or your marriage becomes more fulfilling—that day may never come. Those are fine goals, but if you stake your joy on those things happening, you'll find yourself perpetually frustrated and you'll miss the very blessings God has for you.

God tells us a number of times throughout Scripture that life is short, like a vapor, and we can't count on what will happen in days ahead. "How do you know what will happen tomorrow? For your life is like the morning fog—it's here a little while, then it's gone," says James 4:14 (NLT). "*Soon* life is gone and then we fly away," says David (Ps 90:10, NLT).

While we can't control our circumstances, change the past or make this fast-moving life go slower, we can decide our attitude. We can see the life we have as a gift no matter what our problems or challenges, and live it to the fullest. And we can choose to not miss out on joy *today*, and not put happiness off until everything's "fixed" in our lives and set right the way we want it.

A place to start is speaking to yourself each morning and saying, "This is the day the Lord has made. I will rejoice and be glad in it" (see Ps 118:24).

Then remind yourself throughout the day to celebrate. I have a

Joy is that deep settled confidence that God is in control of every area of my life.

PAUL SAILHAMER

little card on my refrigerator that says, "Celebrate today! I have come that you might have life abundantly!" It reminds me on the darkest days to find something to celebrate: a rosy red and blue Oklahoma sunset; or if it's rainy, the fact that I don't have to water the garden; the richness of God's Word as I read it in the early morning hours; a crocus peeking up in the yard after the cold winter; a letter from a friend; my husband's smile as he comes in the door after work. Each day is a gift, and there's always something to celebrate if you look for it.

One of my favorite poems by William Wordsworth begins, "My heart leaps up when I behold a rainbow in the sky. So was it when I was a child, so be it when I am a man, or let me die." *What makes your heart leap up? What makes you want to jump for joy?*

If it's kite flying (which is one of my personal favorite things to do on a windy day), then go fly a kite. Watch the kite climb higher and higher in the sky and as you let the string out, release all your worries and

I think we can do something which will cause the shortness of life to work in our behalf, rather than against us. We can give our lives away! As the commercial suggests, we can "reach out and touch someone." Instead of holing up in our own four-square world, we can strive to be characterized by generosity.

LUCI SWINDOLL

burdens to the Lord. If it's roses and beautiful flowers that delight you, find a rose garden in your town or a botanical garden to refresh your soul. If it's art, stroll through an art museum on the weekend. If it's outdoor activity, make time to slide down a slide and swing with a child at the park and laugh in the wind or play tennis with a friend. Even on an ordinary day you can take a walk around the block and discover many things to celebrate: the trees, the blue bird serenading you, the people God's planted around you in the neighborhood where you live. Look for the miraculous in daily life: the miracle of a sunrise, a baby's soft skin, even an angelic visitation. Be alert to the blessings and simple pleasures you find in nature and the world around you. Let your heart leap up, and be filled with wonder. Joy will flood in like you won't believe!

Recently, I met a woman who lives with this attitude of celebration and generosity of spirit. Although she's a nurse and mother of three, Peggy's gone on three medical mission trips to Mexico and the Amazon River in South America. She sets up first-aid stations in the community in crisis and is there whenever help is needed. She teaches CPR classes for the American Red Cross. In her spare time she serves as an animal educator, showing zoo animals to school kids, giving tours at the zoo and teaching classes about animals. You'd think this lady would take a break in the summer. But for ten years she's served each summer as a camp nurse for two hundred children. She launched a clown ministry with her youth group. And in her forties she tackled rock climbing and embarks on mountain-climbing adventures with the Sierra Club. What's Peggy's secret to living a joyful, adventurous life?

"The size of your world is the size of your heart" is her motto. She's discovered her heart is happiest exploring, learning and "out on the range" or on the edge of a mountain. What makes her heart leap up is hiking and helping people and tackling new challenges. So she pursues those activities with gusto. "If life isn't an adventure, it's not living at all," she says.

Try something new and find out what makes your heart "leap up." Celebrate life. Look for everyday miracles and reach out to the folks around you. Don't forget to thank God for the gift of today. And please don't put off joy until some magical time when....

Instead, choose joy today!

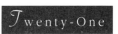

Twenty-One

My wish for you ...
a special letter from me to you.

Here's a letter for you to write with wishes and hopes from your mother's heart—or for daughters to add their own insights to with each passing year.

About the Authors

Cheri Fuller is a popular inspirational speaker and a best-selling author of a dozen books including *When Mothers Pray, When Families Pray, Quiet Whispers From God's Heart for Women, Christmas Treasures of the Heart,* and *Motherhood 101.* Cheri's articles have appeared in *Today's Christian Woman, Family Circle, Spirit-Led Woman, Living With Teenagers* and numerous other magazines. She and her husband have three grown children and one grandchild, and live in Oklahoma City, Oklahoma.

Sandra P. Aldrich is a speaker and author or co-author of twenty books including *Heartprints, The Christian Mom's Answer Book, Bless Your Socks Off: Unleashing the Power of Encouragement,* and *From One Single Mother to Another.* She has written more than five hundred articles in *Focus on the Family, Moody Magazine, Discipleship Journal,* and *Today's Christian Woman.* She is a widow and lives in Colorado Springs, Colorado. She has two grown children.